The River
and the
Wolf
and other stories

*Amy!
Thank you for your support! You are a wonderful, brilliant lady!
Enjoy the read! Each time a story is read the characters live!
Chris Craft*

Christopher Craft

Gracednotes Ministries
405 Northridge St. NW
North Canton, OH 44720

The River and the Wolf and other stories
Copyright © Christopher Craft, 2021

All rights reserved

Printed in the United States

ISBN- 9798474687292

This book is dedicated to Mignon Elma Work Craft, my mother; the first person in my life to firmly believe in the power of creativity.

Acknowledgments

Few human endeavors are accomplished in isolation. And so it has been with the writing of this book. The stories in this work required review and editing. They required the consideration of different perspectives and editorial reviews. The publication of the book needed experienced guidance, a unified format, and technological skill. The free creative process; the driving force of this work, needed nurturing, growth, and direction. All these things required the time and effort of many friends.

It is with great humility I extend sincere appreciation to those people without whom this book could not be published or the writings shared.

I dedicated *The River and the Wolf* to my mother because she was the first person in my life to recognize and to awaken me to the magic, mystery, and majesty of the great gift of human creativity. She was an aspiring author and a dedicated educator. To her my everlasting appreciation.

I met Mr. Wilbur Arnold by chance; on a whim; perhaps a tap on the shoulder telling me to pursue the acquaintance. I answered this call. Wilbur and I became friends of purpose and, together, founded a wonderful arts education program for preschool children that has, and continues to impact the lives of thousands of children.

Wilbur was a genius. It was my association with him and his philosophical challenges that inspired me with the suggestion that I might write.

Mr. David Harding is a retired educator and an active community leader in the City of Massillon, Ohio. I met David through the Massillon Museum, where he serves on the Board of Trustees. Being a man of literature, David was the perfect person to seek an opinion concerning my work. He graciously agreed and has been my trusted editor throughout. He also wrote the Forward for this book. I seriously owe you, David!

I had not the slightest idea about the process of publication. It was suggested that I should contact JoAnn Shade. JoAnn is a published author and has worked with the Massillon Museum on various projects. She has also assisted many potential writers to successfully publish their work. I owe JoAnn a huge "Thank You!"

I am of another generation; I am a Boomer! I know nothing about technology. Fortunately, I work for the Massillon Museum! A philosophy of the Massillon Museum, its Board of Trustees, and its Director, Alex Nicholis Coon, is that the success of the organization depends upon the growth, welfare, and success of its professional staff. A museum is an educational institution dedicated to the expansion of the human mind and the stimulation of the creative human spirit. The true mission of every museum is life-long learning. Massillon Museum lives and thrives because it actively pursues and embodies that philosophy. I appreciate the Museum's support in this endeavor, and its assistance and patience in helping this old Boomer better understand technology and use it to achieve the completion of this work.

To those who willingly read one or more of my stories, and provided their constructive criticism with the intent to improve the work, thank you all. Emily Vigil, Craig May, Ruthann Bosley, John Kiste, John Craft, Joseph Fortunato, and anyone I may have inadvertently not mentioned; your input and perspective have not only improved this end product, but have helped me to become a better writer. Thank you for your patience, honesty, time, and input.

My wife, Marcia Craft, who had to put-up with me as I created this book; who has to put-up with me even when I'm not creating a book. Marcia had to read the rough drafts of each story, and then she had to read the edits, and then the edits of the edits. She had to discuss the characters and the changes in plot even when she had something else she would rather be doing. My love and deepest appreciation is ever and always hers.

Contents

1	Pup	1
2	The River and the Wolf	15
3	The Encounter	37
4	The Facilitator	55
5	Billy	73
6	Teacher	111
7	Sanctuary	175

Foreword

You will actually believe you are there!!

Recently I was afforded the opportunity to serve as a proof reader for Chris Craft's book of short stories. As a retired English professor, I have read thousands of articles and writings . . . and I figured I was in for more of the same. I was totally mistaken.

Chris has the unique ability to blend words and ideas that bring scenes vividly alive for his readers. Whether it be nature . . . or an animal . . . or a moment in time . . .Chris allows all who venture into his prose the opportunity to savor, discover and believe . . . and that speaks volumes about a writer and his craft.

I was the fortunate one. I was able to see and experience these feelings and his world long before others. I was honored to be so invited and so inundated . . . and I thank Chris for venturing forth, taking a chance, fighting the good fight, believing , and producing a piece of literature worthy of respect and acclaim.

Enjoy the book. You will actually believe you are there.

David E. Harding
May 2021

Introduction

In the depths of a dreary winter afternoon, with the Sun setting behind the frozen horizon of your view as you gaze through your living room window; the snow pack takes-on a pale blue hue against the deep shadows of the distant forest. The outside temperature drops quickly in the unrelenting cold of the waning light.

But you are warm. Wrapped tightly in your favorite flannel robe, heavy woolen socks keeping your toes safe from the chill, you are comfortably curled upon a sofa before a crackling fire set in the stone fireplace. On the side table, a box of chocolates and a pot of hot tea are set close by.

In this quiet time, with the long hours of a winter night ahead, it is my wish that these writings bring you enjoyment, escape, and valuable introspection.

Then, someday in the future, after several decades of purpose and joy; your own story finds you digging through an old, dusty, and long forgotten box in basement or attic. Pulling this worn and dirty manuscript from the box and wiping the dust away, you, curiously, decide to take it to a local bookseller's shop.

He, after presenting you his bald pate for some time across the old, worn, stained and pitted counter, as he closely and intently studies the writings and signature through his scratched, Coke-bottle lenses, looks up in astonishment! Gazing at you over the heavy frames of his ancient spectacles, eyes wide and slightly crossed, bushy brows bouncing parenthetically in his excitement, his high wrinkled brow between; he exclaims in a shrill, high-pitched, and wiry voice, "Do you have any idea what you have here?"

Enjoy!

Christopher Craft

1

"Pup"
Autobiographical

"Pup was a good dog. Pup was my dog. Nobody said so; Pup knew it and I knew it and that's all that mattered."

Folks living in the country will tell you; you gotta have a dog, you just do. Folks that have a dog usually have more than one, over time. Every once in a while, one stands out.

Pup was a good dog. Pup was my dog. Nobody said so; Pup knew it and I knew it, and that's all that mattered.

He was a mutt, sired by our border collie "King," out of a stray beagle my dad brought home. I was only six or seven at the time, and remember running out of the house to play two months or so before Pup was born. I came to an immediate stop, staring in shock! I turned right around and ran back into the house shouting, "Mom, the dogs are stuck together!" I couldn't understand why the dogs were stuck together! I understand now.

Pup wasn't much to look at, the runt of a litter of four, all black with one white sock, a white splash on his chest, and a whip tail. He was short-haired and about the size of a beagle, no bigger. I guess you could say he was a black beagle, but stockier.

My dad was always bringing home strays; he just liked animals. I remember him bringing home three Saint Bernard puppies one time. Mom was not happy about that; it took a long time to find homes for them, and they just kept eating and eating and getting bigger and bigger. Dad didn't bring many strays home after that. When I was a kid, there were always animals around: dogs, cats, goats, and poultry.

Mom and Dad raised poultry at one time or the other, to make a little extra cash; chickens, ducks, and turkeys. I don't know if they ever made a profit, but they tried. They also raised goats and sold the milk to a local hospital for babies who couldn't have cow's milk.

There was a platform in the goat shed, built to about waist-high, with a ramp at one end and a post at the other;

to tie up the goat. This was the milking platform. They would lead a goat up the ramp and tie it to the post. Mom could stand there and milk the goat without leaning over, easy as you please. When the pail was full, she would take it to the kitchen where they had a small pasteurizer. Of course, to keep milking the nannies, the nannies had to be fresh and that meant they had to have kids, baby goats. It was the kids that my brothers and sister and I liked most! Kids are always fun, natural clowns, fun to play with, and fun to watch. They're quick, agile, funny, and love to run and jump on things…anything. Today, I'll entertain my granddaughter by typing in "baby goats" on Facebook and watching the posted videos.

• • •

As much fun as the kids were for us, they were a constant source of frustration for our parents. It was nearly impossible to keep them contained. The baby goats seemed to consider every effort my father made to contain them as a challenge, and they always managed to escape. One summer morning, we came out of the house to find three of them standing on the roof of the car, parked in the driveway.

After the litter of puppies was weened, dad gave the beagle and Pup's brothers and sisters to a hunter he knew to be trained as hunting dogs. He kept "Pup." I don't know why. Maybe I asked him to, but I don't remember that. Or maybe he just felt sorry for the little runt.

Pup had another name, a real name. As I write this, I cannot remember what it was. It doesn't matter, really. Everybody called him "Pup" and the name stuck. His father, King, was still with us, and Pup was the only "puppy" we kept from the litter. So, being the "puppy," we just started calling him "Pup." I don't think anyone ever used his real name.

I don't recall Pup playing much; he certainly didn't like playing "fetch." You'd throw the ball and yell "go get it!" He would just lie in the grass and look at you. So, you'd roll the ball right to him and say, "Bring it here, Pup!" He'd sniff it, and then just lay there in the grass, panting and looking at you, probably wondering what was wrong with you.

What Pup did like was adventure: hunting, exploring, going to the woods. I suppose it was the beagle in him.

My parents had eleven acres east of Louisville, in Stark County, northeastern Ohio. Mom and Dad leased seven acres to the neighbor for farming, and raised a garden on about an acre or more. There were two and a half acres of woods: an old apple orchard, the trees too old to be much good, and a strip of scrub locust. Most would call it wasteland, but for us, it was adventure land. We spent a lot of time in that woods, climbing the apple trees, building forts and trails, playing "hide and seek" and cowboys and Indians. And wherever I went and whatever I did, Pup was there, right along with me. He gave away my hiding place more than once.

There was a big apricot tree in the yard next to the house. Dad rigged a porch swing to it by putting one end of a locust log into the elbow of a limb about ten feet up the trunk and the other end at the top crossing of two more locust logs bolted together and set angled apart at the bottom. The family would sit out on, and around, the swing, under that apricot tree on summer evenings. Of course the dogs would join us. When he wasn't doing anything else, Pup would spend a lot of time lying in the grass under that apricot tree. If Pup was not under the tree and the four children were not around, he would be gone; out on an adventure of his own.

During the 50s and 60s, a dog had to have a license, but there were no invisible electric fences to keep dogs from straying off. You could chain your dog, but Dad wouldn't do that. He thought it was a cruel thing to do, and believed it would make a dog mean. There were house dogs, of course, but we lived in the country and most people believed that people lived in houses, not dogs. Mother was a strong advocate of that belief, but Dad was a little softer on it than she was. There were times when Mom was on an errand or away and Dad would be home. He would let the dog into the house for a while, especially in the winter. Mom probably knew the dog, or dogs, had been in the house, either from a lingering odor, or some unexplained black hair swishing across the kitchen floor. But if she suspected anything, she never let on.

Our dogs were outdoor dogs, country dogs; farm dogs. They were fed table scraps and ate well. And there was plenty of straw provided for them to bed down in the barn. I do remember that they were brought in, onto the closed-in back porch, to sleep during especially cold winter nights. But they were never chained.

For a dog with beagle in his blood, this meant freedom: roaming, hunting, exploration; adventure. Pup took every advantage of it. If nothing much was happening around home, or my brothers and sister and I were in school, Pup would roam. He might be gone for the day or he might not show up for two or three days.

• • •

One day in the fall of the year, I came home from school, stepped off the bus, and headed up through the yard toward the house. Pup was lying in his usual spot, under the apricot tree. When he saw me, he struggled to his feet and came hobbling toward me, dragging his front right leg. Something was definitely wrong. He had been out on one of his adventures and had been somewhere he probably should not have been. He had been shot.

We didn't have a lot of money, so taking an animal to the vet just didn't happen. I do not remember why my parents took Pup to the vet, or why they spent the money to try to fix him instead of just putting him to sleep, but they did. Trouble was, he'd been shot with a shotgun; his upper right leg and part of his shoulder bone were shattered. The vet did the best he could, but the bones were so badly damaged, they would never heal right. Pup forlornly hobbled around in a cast for weeks. When the cast was finally removed, the leg was very deformed and Pup could barely use it; he was permanently crippled.

Dogs are very resilient and adaptable creatures and Pup was no exception. He learned to tuck his almost useless right leg up under his chest when he moved and only used it as a prop when he was standing still. The end result: it didn't slow him down one bit. The more he used his good leg, his left leg, the stronger it became. When he walked, he had a little bounce to his pace, as his front end bounced up and down, step to step, from being able to use only one leg. But when he ran, he would tuck that bad leg up to his chest, run low to the ground, reaching out with that powerful good leg, and go faster than when he had been able to use all four legs. I really think the whole experience made him stronger, faster, better.

• • •

Our land was bordered and separated from the neighboring farm by an old, abandoned township road. It served Farmer Lutz, the next-door neighbor, very well as it allowed him easy access to most of his fields. Beyond the fields were farmer Lutz's woods.

Lutz's woods were like another country, far away and mysterious. It was actually only a ten or fifteen acre stand of maple and oak trees, interspersed with open areas of multi-floral rose. The area was pasture for farmer Lutz's cattle, but it was the ultimate adventure for Pup and me. We weren't allowed there often, a couple times a summer, but we would try to sneak off to Lutz's woods whenever we could.

On a summer afternoon of my tenth or twelfth year, the neighbor kid and I went to Lutz's woods. Naturally, Pup and King went along with us. We were walking around the woods, absorbed whatever adventure we had created in our imaginations, when the dogs took off for a big multi-floral rose bush nearby. They started to circle the bush, growling and barking furiously. We couldn't see anything because of the density of the bush, but knew they had cornered some critter. The bush was protection for the critter and a sharp, jagged deterrent for the dogs. In their frustration at their failure to get to the critter, their circling, snarling and barking increased in intensity and ferocity.

Finally, Pup couldn't take it any longer. He barged head-long right into the jagged thorns of the bush, ignoring the scratching and puncturing pain the bush's thorns must have caused him as he disappeared into the center. The snarling, hissing and barking from within the bush immediately went to a whole new level. Suddenly, out backed Pup from the bush. Attached to his muzzle was one of the biggest groundhogs I had ever seen, every bit as big as Pup, maybe bigger! It was hard to tell who had who; their muzzles were intertwined, saliva and blood was flying in all directions as each of them shook their heads to get free of the other. Within half a second, King attacked the monster groundhog from behind.

We stood there in amazement and shock as the viciousness and violence became even more brutal. The poor groundhog fought desperately and bravely for his life, but he had little chance against the two dogs. The dogs, instinctively working together like their wild relatives, were very efficient killers, and with their blood up, the end came quickly. The groundhog rolled over onto his back as they finished him. When it was over, Pup and King circled around, sniffing the body for a while, then lay down and licked their own wounds. Pup was a hard, tough, and fearless little dog.

...

Across the road and up a rise, about two hundred yards north of our house, lived a retired farmer, Norvin Hershberger. His son had taken over his dairy farm, and Norvin had built a small retirement home for his wife and himself on the property. The dairy farm was a fairly big operation, milking nearly one hundred high-quality, registered Holstein cattle. Milking had to be done twice each day, every day, early in the morning and late in the afternoon. It was a big job, and Norvin would walk down to the big dairy barn every morning and every afternoon to help his son do the milking. It was quite a trek because he had to walk the two hundred or so yards down the road to the farm lane across from our house, then another several hundred yards down the lane to the farm buildings.

Being a country man, and a farmer, Norvin owned a dog, a big dog; a very large, pure-bred German shepherd. I never knew that dog's name, but, like most farm dogs in the 50s and 60s, and like Pup, that big German shepherd was not chained up. He, too, was allowed to roam.

One afternoon, my mother and I were in the kitchen, she canning, me doing something kids of twelve or thirteen do. Mom looked out the kitchen window to see Norvin's big German shepherd marking his territory right in the middle of the big, beautiful, European-style flower garden that she had painstakingly created over the course of several years. She immediately ordered me to go out into that garden and chase that "darn dog away before he kills the flowers!" I, being a good son, immediately complied.

Neither one of us had really thought through the situation very well. The German shepherd probably weighed-in at eighty to ninety pounds. At that time in my life, I was a skinny, little, junior high kid, weighing in at only one hundred pounds, or a little more. The German shepherd and I were really not well acquainted, let alone comfortable in each other's company. These things did not cross my mind as I went out the kitchen door, walked across the closed-in porch, stepped out the back door and started down the flagstone walk parallel to the outside kitchen wall between the house and another of my mother's flower gardens.

The possibility that the German shepherd might not take well to me "chasing" him away from his so recently marked territory, or what action he might take in defense of that newly-marked territory, did not cross my mind.

As it was, I need not have been concerned. As I approached the end of the walkway and was about to enter the garden where the "darn dog" had violated my mother's flowers, a black streak blew by my knees so fast as to be but a flash! It was Pup in full, powerful and purposeful sprint. He too was offended by the presence of the German shepherd who was encroaching on his territory. Pup was at full speed and he did not slow, he did not hesitate, he did not try to threaten. He hit that dog at full speed, dead center on his side. Pup was like a torpedo; he knocked the German shepherd off his feet and down. Pup then stood on the dog with his good leg and proceeded to slap him across the face with his crippled leg.

The German shepherd, being nearly three times the size of Pup, was able to squirm from under Pup's strong leg. He jumped up and took off; out of the garden and up the road for home with his tail tucked between his legs, and with Pup practically attached to his flanks. I will never forget the sight of those two dogs running up that road. Pup took that dog home!

After it was over, Pup came back home, went out to the apricot tree, lay down in the grass, and licked his bad leg. It was as though nothing had happened at all; it was merely part of a day's work, no big deal. The German shepherd never came back.

I wonder now, did Pup go after that shepherd because he intruded into Pup's territory? Or was Pup's understanding of what I was about to become involved in with that large dog deeper than my own awareness of the danger of the situation? Was Pup putting himself on the line to protect me? I would like to think that was the case.

• • •

As time does for all of us, the years went quickly by for Pup. His muzzle grew more grey, and he spent more time under the apricot tree. His bad leg bothered him more as he aged and he developed arthritis in the depleted joints. Pup had a unique way of lying down caused by the injury to his leg. The gimp leg could not lie straight, but would angle up and in from the elbow, crossing over his good leg. As he lay on the ground panting, the crossed legs gave him a stately pose, almost as if he was assuming an attitude to have his portrait done by some important animal artist, his crossed legs and grey muzzle creating an air of superiority and wisdom. When he wanted to lay his head down, the bad leg gave him an elevated prop. Pup still went on an adventure from time to time, but they were fewer and he was gone less and home more.

I started high school and my attention was redirected from adventures in the woods to sports, girls, and socializing; the adventures of growing up. I spent less and less time with Pup and rarely went to the woods. My activities at home became more focused on adult chores and responsibilities and there was little time for play.

One day, Pup was gone. He had gone on one of his adventures and he never came home. Maybe he, again, went somewhere he shouldn't have, and wasn't as lucky as he had been the first time he was shot. Maybe he knew his time had come and went off somewhere private, away from people, near the woods he loved, and just went to sleep. We never knew what happened to him. His end was inevitable.

I've had many dogs since Pup. Each has been special in its own way. But Pup was different; Pup was important. Living an active, busy life today, I don't think of him often, but I'll never forget him.

Maybe it's because he was so tough, or maybe because he was my first dog. Perhaps it is because he refused to give-in, to let life get the better of him even though he was a runt and disabled. Pup stoically endured the disadvantages and injuries life dealt him, overcame them, turned them to his advantage, and refused to allow them to define him. Pup chose to live.

Folks living in the country will tell you, you gotta have a dog, you just do. Folks that have a dog usually have more than one, over time. Every once in a while, one stands out.

Pup was a good dog. Pup was my dog. Nobody said so; Pup knew it and I knew it and that's all that mattered.

• • •

What an honor that Man has been so blessed to enjoy such a rich relationship with such a wondrous gift from nature. How unique that two completely different species have maintained a committed and dedicated association for so many millennia (I looked it up, between 16,000 and 32,000 years). How sad the beast cannot enjoy the longevity of Man. How tragic Man cannot match the forthright, bold, and undisguised nobility of the beast.

2

"The River and the Wolf"

Autobiographical

"The wolf? ...dust these decades."
"The river? ...will flow-on long after I have withered with the wolf."

I announced my retirement from an early childhood education program I had co-created and directed through the Massillon Museum. The program had grown exponentially, was financially stable, and in good hands. It was time to move on to something else; a third career if you will. The first was teaching high school for thirty-one years; the second with the Massillon Museum, The Artful Living Program, and as an adjunct with Malone University, in Canton, Ohio.

My announcement to those many who had played a role in making the program an outstanding one, was necessarily brief. It contained some items of interest that I had experienced over the years and indicated that it was time to add to the list. Among the items mentioned was unexpectedly coming face-to-face with a wolf and staring down the beast during an adventure many years before. This attracted several comments, which surprised me. I did not think of it as having been much, nor had it come to mind very often. It certainly had not been a planned occurrence. It happened very quickly, so quickly, in fact, it was over before I had much time to realize what had happened. It was an event far more breath-taking than brave, and truthfully, I am not certain what made me include it in the retirement notification. Actually, these things happen every day, and to many people, right?

The story is this: Sally and I were walking down the sun-dappled country lane, over-arched with old towering pines, and divided down the middle by the inevitable hump of un-mown grass and weeds that characterize little-used lanes around the world. We were heading toward a cabin we had seen from the river. The cabin was about one to two hundred yards from the road that paralleled the river, and blended into the shadows of the deep woods. We were re-living the adventures of the previous three days and observing how someone who might want to be "away from it all" could live here quite nicely.

As we got closer to the cabin, we both began to feel a twinge of dread, for we really did not know what we were going to find. Would we be met by a jolly old hermit with a toothless grin and sun-darkened wrinkles, welcoming our company and wanting us to sit a spell in old, broken-down, New England, bentwood rockers? Or, would we be met with two side-by-side barrels of a 12-gauge shotgun?

It was a worn log cabin, definitely showing neglect; the shingled roof was mostly covered with moss, the logs were faded and split, and the chinking between them was cracked and pitted. It was one floor and built high off the ground with a covered porch across the front from one end of the cabin to the other. The porch, too, needed work; the decking was split at the ends and covered with moss. The porch roof sagged in the middle and, although four or five feet above the ground, there was no railing. Too, no lattice or covering of any kind enclosed the space from the floor to the ground, creating a deep, vast, and dark void.

The closer we got, the quieter we became and the slower we walked. As we came within fifty feet of the cabin, Sally started to say, "You know, maybe we should just forget it and go back to…" That is as far as she got. Suddenly…

I am sorry! I'm getting ahead of myself. I need to start with why Sally and I were there in the first place. And, who is Sally?

• • •

The summer of 1971 was to be a significant influence upon my life. Of greatest importance, I am still alive. I graduated from college in May of '71, and my draft deferment changed immediately to 1-A, and the Vietnam War was still raging. I was the son of a World War II veteran; there would be no draft-dodging, nor did I believe that was the right thing to do. I did attempt to enroll in Navy OCS (Officer Cadet School), with the thought that if I must go, I will choose the way I go. I was not accepted, to the great benefit of the United States Navy. I awaited my notice, and my fate.

This left my wife and I at loose ends as we waited for me to be drafted. We decided we should do something to fill the undetermined time until I received my invitation from Uncle Sam. She had worked at a girl's summer camp in New Hampshire the summer before and had had a wonderful time. We contacted the camp; Camp Marlyn, on Bradly Lake, in Andover, New Hampshire, to see if they had positions for us. They did! My wife would work with the younger girls, and I would teach canoeing and be a tripping counselor. Obviously, I could not be a "cabin counselor" at a girl's summer camp, but, for safety sake, it was deemed judicious to have a male accompany the girls on trips away from camp. During four or five weekends of the eight-week season, I was to plan, organize, and accompany selected groups of campers and their cabin counselors on canoe trips and back-packing trips in the mountains. For this dream situation, I would be paid!

Although small compared to most other states, New Hampshire is an outdoor wonderland. The Connecticut River borders on the west, with Vermont's Green Mountains just beyond, and on the east lay the sea coast of Maine and the Atlantic. Within its boundaries is the reality of the iconic calendar pictures of New England: wide, rock-strewn streams of rushing, crystal water; hundreds of lakes surrounded by tall pines with water clear enough to see to the bottom. In the north are the White Mountains, peaked and rugged, with Mt. Washington, at over six thousand feet, the highest in the northeastern United States. It is said that Mt. Washington's summit was the first land to be seen by many explorers and immigrants approaching New England from Europe. Within this setting, we would spend the summer.

I was somewhat qualified and prepared for my new position, as I had been a Boy Scout and new basic camping skills. I owned a canoe and had some experience in how to use it on Ohio lakes. However, the camp owners asked me to attend a "white-water school" the week prior to the opening of camp; it was a wise move on their part. I discovered the advantages of the "draw" and "cross-draw" paddle strokes from the front, or bow, of the canoe in navigating white water. I learned to "read" the river; to see the currents and to choose the best course through the rocks; following the deepest flow. I was amazed to discover that one can travel upstream in a strong river current by using the eddies along the edges of the riverbed, swirls and whirlpools created by the friction of the water flowing against the streambed.

I learned that a sixty-pound, aluminum canoe will "breach" (turn sideways) in a ten-mile-per-hour current. When filled with water; it generates approximately two tons of force if driven against an exposed rock by the rushing water. The result is the shockingly instantaneous destruction of the canoe as it crushes against the rock and the two ends are wrapped around the rock into the shape of a hairpin. If you are thrown from a canoe in such a situation, it is in your best interest to be upstream of the canoe and not between it and the rock.

• • •

Camp Marlyn was a wonderful place, an old New England farm repurposed as a summer camp located a mile or so from Andover, along the east side of Bradley Lake. The owners lived in the farm house down the lane from the village. Another lane wound its way several hundred yards through a large stand of old pine to the camp itself. There was a main lodge in an open area on a rise above the lake, which housed the kitchen, dining area, and counselors' work room and lounge, plus a couple of classrooms where the campers had art classes and created projects on rainy days. Down the rise from the main lodge, set within the stand of pine, were six or eight campers' cabins; one for each age group of campers, each with bunk beds for eight or ten campers. A separate, small, private room provided privacy for the cabin counselor.

Each cabin, like everything else owned by the camp, was painted a deep Kelly green, and had large screened-in windows along each side with a wooden cover, hinged at the top. When raining, the cover could be swung out to act as a kind-of porch roof over the window, keeping the rain out and allowing the breeze to flow through the cabin.

At one end of the group of cabins was the library. It was just another cabin, but larger, and filled with shelves of books rather than bunk beds. There was a screened-in covered porch at one end, overlooking the lake, furnished with comfortable seating and end tables with lamps, perfect for a rainy afternoon of reading. I spent more than my share of time there.

Next to the main lodge was the tripping cabin. It was very similar to the campers' cabins, a bit smaller and filled with shelves of camping equipment: tents, backpacks, sleeping bags, cooking utensils, and a plethora of small, interesting items designed to meet the basic needs of outdoor living in the mid-twentieth century. This was my bailiwick and my responsibility. I spent a great deal of time taking inventory, organizing and reorganizing in preparation for weekend canoe and mountain trips.

I would start planning a weekend trip on Wednesday or Thursday, getting the needed materials together, depending upon the length of the trip and the number of girls going. My other responsibility was teaching canoeing. This took place several times each week and occurred at the landing along Bradly Lake.

A large U-shaped dock outlined the swimming area; the younger campers could not go beyond the float rope that connected to two ends of the "U." Swimming classes happened all the time, being one of the primary foci of the camp curriculum. All canoes and watercraft were next to the swimming docks. I taught canoeing to the campers by age group; classes occupying an hour or so of my time each afternoon. If I was not teaching canoeing or preparing for a trip, I was free to explore.

Camp Marlyn owned a large tract of land along Bradly Lake at that time. Today, much of the lake is surrounded by private cabins and camps. In 1971, the lake shore and some distance inland was forest and I often would paddle across the lake to explore the woods on the other side. I was amazed to find a "King's Pine" growing still, on camp property. A massive white pine, perhaps four feet in diameter and two hundred feet in height, apparently several hundred years old. During the eighteenth century, as timber became increasingly in short supply in England, the Royal Navy demanded ever more timber for the ships needed to maintain its ocean empire. Agents of the Empire circulated throughout New England, searching for the best and the tallest timber. These would be designated "Kings Pines," not to be cut or touched by any but the King's shipbuilders, and used for masts on the great ships-of-the-line.

We conducted several mountain trips that summer. One-day trips for the younger campers: Mt Ascutney, just west of the Connecticut River, and Mt. Kearsarge, just several miles to the west of Andover. Kearsarge, a low peaked mountain of about three thousand feet, dominated the horizon to the west of Camp Marlyn and reflected on the surface of Bradly Lake as one looked at it from the waterfront. The view was present throughout the camp and was one of those iconic calendar pictures of New England. Residents took it for granted because it was always there but many would be willing to spend a fortune for that view from the deck of their home.

Smaller groups of older campers went on multiple-day climbs in the White Mountains to the north. One trip was to climb Mt. Washington, a small mountain by world standards, but a deadly dangerous mountain if not respected. A longer trip, for the older campers, was to climb the Falling Waters Trail, up and across three peaks of the Franconia Range: Little Haystack (4,800 ft.), Mt. Lincoln (5,100 ft.), and Mt. Lafayette (5,300 ft.). This was a challenging but grand and magnificent hike. Once at the top of the climb, the trail follows the saddlebacks of the ridge, from one peak to the next. Hikers can easily see down the steep slopes in both directions, as the mountains descend into the narrow valleys, locally known as the notches, then ascend up the blue-green slopes of the neighboring ridges with the rocky peaks and crags above.

On each of these trips, I was accompanied by the cabin counselor and their campers, but I was not the only "tripping counselor." Sally Booker also went on nearly every trip taken by Camp Marlyn campers, and had for many previous years, back to the time when she was a camper. In her early twenties, Sally was an institution at Camp Marlyn; in some ways, she was Camp Marlyn. She was a cabin counselor, tripping counselor, and taught camp-craft. The older campers had known Sally for several years and absolutely loved her.

She was a native New England girl and had graduated from the University of New Hampshire. A bit of a tomboy, she kept her disheveled, sandy-colored hair cut short, so she didn't need to waste her time fixing it every morning. She wore no makeup, nor did she need to; she was quite attractive, tall and lanky, with a bit of an angular face and brown eyes. Her most attractive feature was her smile. Her face fairly beamed with life when she laughed, and she laughed often. She was a serious outdoor-girl, and had climbed most of the mountains in the White Mountain range, some of them several times. She had already worn-out several pair of hiking boots, and the pair she wore that summer were at their limit. She knew things about the outdoors then, I still have yet to learn. I admired her, and depended upon her greatly.

We went on one fabulous canoe trip that summer; a four-day, white-water trip on the upper Androscoggin River, south of Errol, New Hampshire. This trip was for the older campers; the sixteen to seventeen-year-olds. This would be their last year as campers and this was to be their memorable reward for their many summers of loyally attending Camp Marlyn. There were six of them, their names have faded from memory over the years. Sally and I would round out this team of adventurers. Three campers would be in each of two canoes, with some supplies. Sally and I would be in the third canoe, with the bulk of the camping equipment.

Camp Marlyn owned an old Chevy Suburban, green of course, but washed-out and faded. Upon its roof, we placed two canoes, side-by-side. The third rested between, and on top, of the first two, making an odd, attention-getting sight as we drove north to our launch site. The six campers, Sally and I rode in the Suburban, followed by the owners in their pick-up truck with most of our gear in the bed. Once they dropped us off at our launch site, they drove both the Suburban and the pick-up back to camp, leaving us to our own devices.

The one hundred and seventy mile length of the Androscoggin River flows south through northern New Hampshire, then turns east into Maine where it flows into the Kennebec River and on to the Atlantic. In years past, it was a logging river, and was dammed at several places to control the flow, allowing innumerable thousands of logs to float south to the paper mills of Berlin and Gorham.

During the 1960s and 70s, it was a favorite of white-water thrill-seekers and adventurers as the water flowed through the dams creating medium-level rapids below. As the river banks narrowed, the turbulent water accelerated its crashing course over the rocky riverbed, and as the banks widened, the water spread and the current slowed. The result was intermittent rapids of fifty to several hundred yards, some quite violent, interspersed with long stretches of calm.

I have canoed since this trip on the Androscoggin, but only occasionally. The tame lakes and rivers of Ohio offer nothing in comparison to the experience of those few days on the Androscoggin. I have white-water rafted on Pennsylvania's Youghiogheny River and enjoyed the thrill, but nothing has even approached the experience of that trip down the Androscoggin during the summer of '71. Each day consisted of rising to make a fire and breakfast, followed by miles of the river through the wilderness, mostly floating easily along, and then brought to anticipated awareness as a stretch of white-water would appear around a bend, the crashing water heard before it was seen.

Then the roar of the water, the splash of the cold as the spray flew over the canoe, the thrill of the canoe picking up speed and rushing past rocks, following the depth of the current. "Draw! Draw! Cross-draw! Watch the sharp rock to the left! See it?! Draw! Draw!" There was always the edge of not knowing what would happen if things went wrong, if your draw stroke mistakenly sent the canoe into the wrong flow, or if you hit a shallow rock you didn't see.

We would pull out for lunch and sit along the shoreline, eating peanut-butter and jelly sandwiches and drinking "bug juice" (Kool-Aid). At night, we would put up our tents, build a fire and have trail stew or "biscuits on a stick" with butter, and talk or tell ghost stories until well after dark. We saw not another human being the entire trip, and, but for the moose standing in the water on the other side of the river I saw early one morning, not another living being. The experience was idyllic.

Late morning of the last day, as we floated lazily along, each thinking of the impending end of this great trip, we heard an unusually loud roar ahead. We gathered ourselves together and prepared to shoot another rapid. As we got closer we could see ahead that this stretch of white-water was more than we had been through before. With some concern, Sally indicated to pull to the bank so we could assess what was ahead, and mentally map the route before we entered the turbulence. The rapids were about two hundred to three hundred yards long and far more intense than any we had been through before. We decided to try them without carrying the gear and spent the next hour portaging it down to the bottom of the violent stretch of river. We returned to the head of the rapids, got into our canoes and pushed off into the current. Sally and I went first, followed by the two canoes with the campers; their strict instructions were to follow our path exactly. I was in the bow, Sally in the stern.

Not long after, the three canoes were rafted together at the end of the white-water, half filled with water, and with all eight of us completely soaked and grinning ear to ear! WHAT A RIDE!! I have never done anything as thrilling in my life since. It was beyond description! "LET'S DO IT AGAIN!!"

We quickly beached the canoes and carried, dragged, and huffed and puffed them back to the top of the frenzied stretch of water. We put in the canoes, excitedly jumped in and pushed off. Sally and I paddled toward the same path of descent as our first trip, but we misjudged our course and missed our first, planned mark. We were no longer on our mapped course and were frantically steering a new one. Halfway down the churning rapids, we shot out over a drop, a very large rock with water flowing over and around it, creating a deep hollow on the down side of the rock. To this day, I remember looking down from the bow of the canoe, thinking the drop was a long way down; far below the reach of my paddle, possibly three or four feet below the bottom of the boat. We were moving very fast and fully half the canoe was over the drop before we fell. The bow immediately went under.

I do not remember the next few seconds. I know I was under water, despite wearing a life vest. When I resurfaced and became aware of my surroundings, the canoe had breached and filled with water. It was now going down the rapids sideways and my face was against its side. I put my elbows up on the gunnel and pulled my head above the side of the canoe. Sally was holding onto the other side looking at me, her hair plastered to her head, mouth open, and her eyes big and staring. I instantly realized why a look of shock was on her face; I was in big trouble. I was on the down side of a breached aluminum canoe in a ten-mile-per-hour current! I was faced up river, the swamped canoe pushing me downstream. I could feel my legs dragging along under the canoe and bouncing along the rocks on the bottom of the stream! If the canoe hit a large rock sticking out above the surface of the water, I would be crushed!

I reached my left arm over to the right and tried to pull myself toward the end of the canoe with both hands. No luck: I couldn't move at all against the pressure of the boat forcing me downstream. I tried pulling myself in the other direction, but with the same result. Maybe, if I took off my life vest, I could go under the boat. But I quickly discovered there was no way I could reach and unfasten the clasps as the force of the water pushing the boat against my chest trapped the life vest clasps between me and the canoe's side. With the vest on, I couldn't move!

There was nothing I could do; I was along for a very dangerous ride. My legs bounced along under the boat, the water sloshed over me while we made our way down the rapids. Sally stared at me across the canoe, I stared back; completely helpless, totally at the mercy of the river. With nothing else to do, we rode the rapids until the end. I remember feeling no fear, just resignation. It did not take long; five minutes, less. There was no guiding us, for the current carried the canoe. We crashed along, staring at each other, the swamped canoe between us. There was no point in trying to talk; we would not be able to hear each other over the roar of the river, even though we were only three feet apart.

Finally, the current slowed, the roar subsided, and we entered the calm.

Sally started screaming, "Are you okay!? Oh my God! Are you sure you're okay? Oh, my God!"

I didn't say anything; I just kept hanging onto the side of the canoe, staring at Sally.

She kept screaming, "Oh, my God! Oh, my God! Oh, my God!!"

Our vignette was finally interrupted by the first canoe of campers, who had shot the rapids without incident, and had seen what had happened. They frantically paddled to us and asked if we were all right. I stopped shaking and answered, "We're fine!"

I looked back to Sally, who had calmed down as well and said, "Let's flip the canoe." We did, handily, and climbed in.

By this time, the second camper canoe came up and wanted to know what had happened. We spent the next ten minutes relating the incident, with many "Oh my Gods" thrown in; Sally and I talking in less than firm tones, the campers, with all eyes and mouths agape. After having a little time to catch our breath, settle our nerves, and reassure the campers again that we were fine, we pulled to the shore and loaded our gear, then paddled on, downstream. No one suggested shooting that stretch of rapids a third time. It was a quiet trip the rest of that afternoon.

The river paralleled the road along the final hours of the trip, sometimes close enough to see, other times, several hundred yards away. We had made arrangements with the owners to pick us up near the highway along this length of the river on the next morning. We would camp fairly close to the road and be ready for them about mid-morning the next day.

Late in the afternoon, we started looking for a good spot to camp, close to the road, but not too close. We figured we would be up and packed by ten in the morning and would be able to flag down the owners as they drove by, looking for us. We found a great campsite only a hundred feet or so from the road, level, with plenty of room for the tents, and with ample firewood to be gathered with little effort. The site was hidden from the road by high brush, so we would not attract any unwanted attention. While checking it out, Sally noticed a driveway on the other side of the highway, leading back into the deep forest of pine and suggested we might check with the owners to make certain it would be fine to camp here, just to be safe.

We instructed the campers to setup their tents, gather wood, and start a fire. We would check with the people down the lane to make sure we weren't trespassing and be right back. We crossed the highway and started down the lane. It was a typical country lane, over-arched with old towering pines and divided down the middle by the inevitable hump of unmown grass and weeds that characterize little-used country lanes around the world. As we walked, we began to see a cabin about two hundred yards from the road. It blended into the shadows of the deep woods. We were re-living the adventures of the last three days, especially our close call in the rapids earlier in the afternoon. We observed that someone who wanted to be "away from it all" could live here quite nicely.

As we got closer to the cabin, we both began to feel a twinge of dread; we really did not know what we were going to find. Would we be met by a jolly old hermit with a toothless grin and sun-darkened wrinkles, welcoming our company and wanting us to sit a spell in old, broken-down, New England, bentwood rockers? Or, would we be met with two side-by-side barrels of a 12-gauge shotgun?

The cabin was an old worn log cabin, definitely showing neglect. The shingled roof was mostly covered with moss, the logs were faded and split, and the chinking between them was cracked and pitted. Only one story, it was built high, allowing a covered porch across the front from one end of the cabin to the other. The porch, too, needed work; the decking was split at the ends and covered with moss. The porch roof sagged in the middle and although the porch was four or five feet above the ground, there was no railing. No lattice or covering of any kind enclosed the space from the decking to the ground, creating a deep, vast and dark void.

The closer we got, the quieter we became, and the slower we walked. This place was definitely not inviting. I was beginning to wonder if anyone actually lived there. As we came within fifty feet of the cabin, Sally started to say, "You know, maybe we should just forget it and go back to…" That was as far as she got.

Out from under the porch; out from the deep, vast blackness of the void exploded…a massive beast! It was huge, but very, very fast! Before we could think, it was to us, and stopped not two feet in front of me. Sally was gone; at some point in those very few seconds, I felt more than heard, or saw, her go. I was alone to face the beast.

I stood my ground, not because I thought to do so, but because I was too shocked to run; I was frozen in place! The face of the beast seemed to be no more than a foot from mine; and though its neck arched-down and its head drooped, it seemed I was staring right into its eyes. The angry arched brows shadowed evil yellow-brown irises punctured by black pupils. The jowls of its muzzle were wrinkled up to expose great, long, dripping canines. Its black and grey ruffed and mottled fur stood on end. I heard a low, deep, quiet growl as it faced me, every muscle in its body rippled; tensed; ready to erupt in vicious violence…against me!

The time needed to absorb all this was only a second. I had no time to think what I might do or what to expect from the animal; no time at all. I'm certain now, that if I had moved, it would have attacked.

A command came from the porch; a human voice, I couldn't tell if it was man or woman. It was a sharp sound, a word...unintelligible. Immediately, the animal backed off and sat, licking the saliva from its dripping mouth. The low growl continued and the heavy-browed, yellow-eyed stare never wavered from my face. I didn't move.

"Good thing ya didn' run, he'da had ya," said the voice.

"Hello!" I replied. I wanted to look to see who the voice belonged to, but sensed not to let my eyes leave the animal. "What kind of dog is it?"

"Ain't a dog; wolf...timber wolf...full bred," the voice replied emphatically.

"Oh... big," I said in a very weak "Oh shit" tone.

"Yep! Waddya want?"

"Uh...we're on a canoe trip, eight of us; get picked-up tomorrow. Would it be okay if we camp along the river the other side of the road tonight?"

"Do whatcha want, I don' care. Don't come back here though. I might not be on the porch next time."

"K, no problem, thanks!"

"Don' turn away from 'im! Back away."

"K, thanks!"

The voice did not reply.

Back away I did, a long way. The wolf watched me go, never took its eyes off me. I backed and backed. Finally, thinking I was far enough away; that it would be safe, I turned away from the beast. I'd backed nearly half the way to the road.

When I got back to camp, Sally started screaming, "Oh my God, Oh my God! What was that?!

"A wolf," I said, sitting down and staring across the river.

"Oh my God! I've never been so scared in my life!"

"Jesus," I murmured.

• • •

The next morning, we all sat by the road waiting to flag down the owners when they came. We had already had breakfast, broke camp and packed all the gear. Then we went up and sat along the road to wait to get picked up. About mid-morning, as expected, here they came with the green camp pick-up and the old green Suburban. We loaded the gear in the truck and fastened the canoes to the top of the Suburban; two on the roof, side by side, the third in the middle, on top of the other two. Camp Marlyn was three hours south.

With the summer over and the campers gone after innumerable tearful hugs and goodbyes, my wife and I returned to Ohio. Nixon ended the draft lottery, so, with greater certainty, we turned our focus to new chapters in our futures. We never saw Sally again, or anyone from Camp Marlyn. There were Christmas cards and letters, but, year by year, they became more occasional. There were memories of faces with names, then faces with names forgotten, and associations faded.

I could have died that summer, in the river. But, I didn't. I could have been seriously injured by the wolf. But, I wasn't. And, over the years, other things happened, other events, other close calls; scrapes with near death. Two others, actually, plus surviving cancer. And the question arises, as it does for most survivors, "Why?"

Why did I survive when so many are dying all around the world, of myriad causes?

Am I intended for some purpose I have yet to accomplish?

"Why?"

It has colored my life, influenced my attitudes, pushed my being, focused my purpose. I have determined to live, to experience, to see, to learn, to understand. And though I am certainly not anyone special, I have been given multiple creative gifts and I am trying to use them to their greatest benefit.

The wolf? ...dust these decades. He does not occupy my mind much, but when he does, his presence, his power, seems so clear as to have faced me just now; his glaring, yellow-brown irises punctured by black pupils and shadowed by arched eyelids, lips curled to expose his teeth; evil in his apparition. Had I run he may not have been able to kill me, as his master would have intervened but he would have done serious damage.

How poignant the tangent meeting of our two lives;

The wolf with the present, over-powering, physical force, yet restrained.

I, the weakest; still, the symbol of near extinction for his kind.

The river? ...will flow on, long after I have withered with the wolf.

3

"The Encounter"
Fiction

"Heh! Heh! Heh!"

It was an absolutely gorgeous spring morning. Temperatures were forecast to be in the upper sixties, unusually warm for an Ohio day in late March. It was already in the mid-fifties, and Jason was enjoying the warmth of the sun as it crested range after range of forest-covered hills. He was standing on the deck of his rustic and secluded log and brick home, perched upon a carefully chosen hilltop in the rolling hills of Carroll County, Ohio. With a cup of freshly brewed coffee in hand, leaning against the deck railing, he let his mind ruminate on the unwarranted negative reputation of living in Ohio. He was a native, born and raised, and would live nowhere else. He enjoyed the changing seasons and appreciated the fact that the negative idea of living here allowed him to have the view he now enjoyed; it kept people away.

Jason Daniel Edmonton was a hugely successful novelist and essayist. The son of two career educators, he graduated high school from a small, consolidated public school district (which employed an excellent English grammar and literature teacher), about fifty miles northwest from where he now stood. His undergraduate degree was from the highly ranked College of Wooster. His masters in American Literature and Creative Writing was from the University of Akron. At sixty-five years old, he counted his life a success. He had two adult children, also enjoying success in their chosen careers, and five beautiful grandchildren. He attributed his tremendous luck in life to his beautiful wife of nearly forty years, Marsha, whom he had met during his Master's program at Akron University.

She was now on an annual, long weekend getaway in Columbus with four of her college buddies. This left Jason a weekend bachelor, and he was looking forward to it as he continued to watch the morning Sun's ascent. He had only one responsibility for the next three days; an interview with a reporter for the Cleveland Fox News affiliate, this afternoon; Friday, at a mutually chosen restaurant in Akron. Other than that, he anticipated a relaxing weekend reading, eating food that Marsha would not approve of, and watching old war movies that Marsha would not watch. There would be several hours of writing, as his publishers were pressing for the next five-chapter installment on his latest novel, and he had yet to write the promised educational essay for the Ohio Department of Education. But for now, Jason was focused on a three-mile walk on the local walking trail that passed within a couple of miles of the house.

He finished his coffee, went into the house and changed into sweats, grabbed his wallet and keys, and headed for the 2008 Jeep Wrangler parked in the driveway. Though beat-up and rusty, of their four cars, the Wrangler was his favorite; he could go anywhere with it. And it came-in very handy on icy winter days in Ohio. The half-mile driveway, winding up and down the steep, wooded hill could be a real challenge in snow and ice, making the Jeep very handy indeed.

As he wound his way through the woods to the entry gate at the bottom of the hill, his thoughts went to the dream he had had the night before. He could not remember much about it, but he certainly remembered that it was not pleasant. As he punched the garage door opener to swing open the security gate, he wondered if the dream was a result of the graphic violence in last night's war movie. He sat at the open gate thinking about the origins of, and explanations for, dreams: were they psychological reactions to former biological events…physiological? Did they occur in reaction to long forgotten life experiences resurfacing in the conscious mind? Did the occurrence of one parallel universe coming in tangential contact with another act as a catalyst, prompting a cross-over of related events?

Or were they, as Scrooge posed in Dickens's *A Christmas Carol,* "...an undigested bit of beef, a blot of mustard, a crumb of cheese...?"

Jason sat considering these things at the open privacy gate another fifteen minutes. This was a familiar process to him; he often spent time mentally focused on ethereal topics, asking himself questions, oblivious to events going on around him. Occasionally, he carried the process further by researching the topic that had captured his attention. He had learned to trust and value these episodes; they often became the foundation for themes and story lines in his novels.

After a while, he became aware of the open gate and of his purpose for driving the Jeep to the bottom of the hill. He pulled forward, looked both ways, and turned left down the county road in the direction of the walking path. As the Jeep picked up speed, Jason clicked the opener to the security gate and glanced into the rear-view mirror to make sure the gate swung shut. The gate was not fancy nor ostentatious, but very utilitarian, merely a high-grade farm gate.

Since Jason published his first best-seller, he had become very security-minded. Only close friends and family were invited to the house on the hill. This also explained scheduling the interview with the Fox reporter in Akron. The reporter was very willing to drive the hour and a half from Cleveland to Jason's home, but Jason firmly nixed that; he had no interest in bringing a journalist into his private lair.

It was only a couple miles to the walking path, and he refocused his mind back to considering the possibility of dreams during the short drive. There could be a myriad of story lines around the topic, and, because dreams are not required to adhere to the laws of nature, physics, or Man, story lines could be wide-open to the wanderings of an uninhibited imagination. The possibilities were truly endless. Jason resolved to do a bit of research into the subject as soon as he finished his morning constitutional. As he pulled into the parking area off the county road and parked the Jeep, he determined that he would also contact a few psychology professors and researchers on the subject and pick their minds.

As he got out of the Jeep and did a few stretching exercises, he noticed that his was the only car in the lot. Well, it was early, and Friday, a work day. The trail would undoubtedly populate as the day went on. Also, there might be others out biking, running, or walking, who had parked in other lots. The trail intersected other roads along its course, every mile or so, and nearly every intersection had a parking area. Still, it would be nicer not to have to smile and nod, or greet everyone he met along the way. It was not that he was unsociable; it was that he enjoyed these walks to work out solutions for his stories. Greeting people interrupted his focus.

The trail was an old railroad spur that had, at one time, connected small, independent coal mines to the main line tracks, allowing the mines to market their product to distant customers. The several coal mines the tracks served had been out-of-business for nearly a century and the tracks had been abandoned for as long. The railroad had pulled up the rails many years ago and let the old wooden ties lie and rot away. A community-minded group had seen the possibility for repurposing the rail bed around the turn of the new century. With the help of local and state representatives, donations, and grants, they had purchased the land and cleared the old right-of-way of debris.

Almost twenty years later, the trail upkeep was becoming problematic. The original community group had lost steam. Grants and donation funding were spotty at best, and the eight-mile trail was showing wear and pot-holes. At places where heavy use really damaged the trail, users or sympathetic farmers would affect temporary repairs. The trail was popular and generally usable throughout its length, but one did need to watch one's step in some stretches.

Jason locked the Jeep, checked his watch so he could see how long his walk would take, and headed down the trail at a firm, healthy walking pace. The trail followed along the valley between two hills and along a stream. It was tree-lined its entire length. Beyond the trees was a varied landscape; farmers' fields lined the trail at various intervals, interspersed with large tracts of timber. The stream accompanied the trail nearly its whole length, sometimes running parallel with it, sometimes winding away into the woods, just to return several hundred yards further on and pass under the trail that bridged it. The stream entered a swampy area about one and a half miles from where Jason parked. The swamp then transitioned into a pond of several acres a little farther along. Some walkers would bring fishing equipment, or a picnic lunch, and stop for a while along the banks of the pond to fish or enjoy the surroundings.

Jason and Marsha enjoyed walking the trail together in the early evenings during the late spring, summer, and fall. Besides being good exercise, it was a good time to share the events of their day, talk about the kids and grandkids, and make plans for new travel adventures. Jason would often walk the trail alone in the mornings after Marsha left for work. If he got to the trail early enough, he would be rewarded by the presence of wildlife along its length.

Among the beauties of the trail was the annual change of seasons. The trail gave an almost sensual immersion into the seasonal changes with their colors, light and shadows, odors, temperatures, and sounds. Like many Ohioans, the love of seasonal changes was among the factors that commanded Jason's and Marsha's loyalty to the state.

Thoughts of all these things ran their course through Jason's mind as he proceeded down the path. He often let his creativity have full freedom when he walked here, but he also made a point of being aware of, and in touch with, the temporal and natural environment, which was always a reliable source for literary expression.

• • •

He was thoroughly enjoying the day as he listened to the stream, swollen by early spring rains, wash along next to him. Ahead was the pond, visible as he passed the next bend in the trail. He began to think about how far he should go before heading back; he did want some time to research dreams, and he had to plan when to start getting ready for the trip to Akron for the meeting with the reporter; the drive would take over an hour. He decided he had better turn around at the pond.

He had encountered no other walkers this morning, but as the pond came into view, he noticed a man standing along the trail near the water. The man wasn't walking, so Jason assumed he must have come out early to do a little fishing. As he walked closer, he realized the man was not moving in any way, but standing there, statuesque, nor was any fishing equipment apparent. As he got even closer, he noticed the man seemed oddly dressed. Partially dressed would be a better way of expressing it. He appeared to be wearing old-fashioned, striped bib overalls. But under the overalls, he was not wearing a shirt. The temperature was unseasonably warm, but not that warm.

Curious, he walked to where the man was standing. As he approached, he noticed the man held a leash, or rather, a length of twine, the other end of which was around the neck of a little black dog. Closer now, he saw that the man appeared to be quite old and, despite his years, unusually tall and erect. Now concerned, he decided he better make sure the old man was not in some kind of distress.

As he came close, the man did not notice him or turn in his direction, so he called out, "Good morning!"

The oddest thing then happened; the man not so much turned toward him, but rather...transitioned...to face Jason. At the same instant, Jason had the sensation that the temperature dropped noticeably; a chill passed over him. And, as Jason now saw the man's face, he stopped dead where he was, his mouth dropping open in shock.

The man was tall, perhaps six foot five inches, possibly more. He was wearing old-fashioned bib overalls, without a shirt under them, as Jason had earlier noticed. But his face…his face! His head seemed unusually big, even for his height, and very round. His hair was pure white, and formed a halo-like image around his head from ear to ear, hanging in strings to his shoulders. The top of his head was completely bald. A long, sharp, pointed nose shadowed an equally long, narrow mouth that seemed to extend nearly to his ears. Both his eyes were absolutely wide-open and completely white, fully covered with cataracts! He had to be totally blind! He had heavy, uncontrolled eyebrows the color of his hair.

But his face…his face! Jason had never seen another human being with so wrinkled a face, with skin nearly as white as his hair. It made Jason think what his own hand might be like if he immersed it in cold water too long. In combination, the man's features, and the white, wrinkled skin, created an apparition beyond anything Jason could ever have imagined; absolutely frightening! He approached no closer.

Jason then noticed that the man was utterly filthy. As Jason's eyes panned down the specter before him, he was shocked to see the man was also barefoot. His bony, pure-white feet were filthy and his toe-nails, all of them, were black, not from dirt under them, but as though they were dead and about to fall off! Jason then jumped slightly, in greater shock! The man was standing in a puddle of water. A puddle formed not from rain, but from the dripping of water off the man himself. Jason now noticed that the man's coveralls and his hair were dripping wet. In fact, as Jason now looked back to the man's face, a drop of water formed and fell from the tip of the man's nose.

"Sir. Are you all right?" he blurted instinctively, and took a concerned step toward the man. At this, the little, black dog, to which Jason had given little notice, stood and emitted a low, protective growl. Jason's attention was immediately drawn to the dog, arresting any further movement toward the man.

The little dog was attached to the man by a dripping, filthy, frayed length of twine. The dog was truly small; perhaps less than ten pounds, but its head was oversized for its body and with a long muzzle.

Jason muttered a barely audible, "Oh, my god!"…as he noticed that the dog's eyes, like the man's, were pure white and completely covered with cataract material. The dog's coat of black fur was dull, mottled and matted, and covered a bony, emaciated body. He could not attach a breed to the dog, and was so disturbed by the nasty appearance of the canine; he wondered that it was diseased. It had not a tail, and seemed to be lacking ears as well. Its lips were curled, revealing pure-white, thin, long, irregular teeth; nothing like normal canine teeth, but more like those of a carnivorous fish from the deepest depths of the sea.

It, too, was standing in a puddle of its own making; its coat soaked and dripping. The image of the black, oversized head of the dog, with the pure white eyes and long, scraggly, sharp teeth, again sent a chill through Jason. What was this animal!?

He again noticed the dropping temperature, and folded his arms over his chest to stop the chill. Looking back to the man's grotesque visage, again he stammered, "Are you all right?"

The man's thin, lipless mouth opened and stretched into a grin that filled Jason with shocking dread. "Heh, heh, heh…" in a raspy, sigh-like voice, was all the reply that emerged from him. And now Jason could see his teeth; a perfect row of small, absolutely white teeth, with no difference in size, front to back, and more of them than there ought to be. In fact, the teeth were tiny, and they grew from exposed gums that were as black and necrotic looking as the man's toenails.

"Who are you?" Jason asked, backing away several steps, his voice going to a high pitch.

The raspy, sighing, "Heh, heh, heh…" was again the sole reply.

"Why are you wet; did you fall into the lake?" Jason was now desperately trying to keep himself under control and bring some normalcy to the encounter. He realized, too, that it had become very cold, and he was beginning to shiver.

Again…"Heh, heh, heh" came the raspy, sigh-sounding response from the wide, teeth-lined grin mounted under the long, thin nose.

Jason studied the bald head, the white wrinkled face with the cataract-covered eyes. He looked again at the diseased, evil looking black dog, still lowly growling at him; with its over-long, thin, sharp teeth dripping saliva into the puddle. This truly was not normal!. The man, the dog, the sudden chill in the air was really quite frightening. Without actually thinking it, Jason determined that it was time to leave; to get away…now!

Jason quickly turned and began to walk away from the unearthly sight behind him, totally shaken by the encounter with the man and shivering almost uncontrollably from what now seemed to be freezing temperatures. He went several yards from the scene and then looked back over his shoulder to make sure the man and dog were not following him. He jerked to a stop, spinning back in the direction he had come!

"OOOHH!!" he let out, now completely terrified, staring back to where the man and dog had been. The emaciated dog still stood in its puddle, teeth exposed. But the man had disappeared. In his place stood another dog; a duplicate. A twin. A second black, diseased and emaciated dog, its head too big, it eyes pure white, its lips curled, with teeth too long, and thin, and white, and sharp, and dripping!

Jason turned and he ran.

At sixty-five, he was not used to running. After what seemed to be at least five minutes and several hundred yards of running, he had to stop and catch his breath. He leaned over with his hands on his knees, breathing hard. He knew he had to have run well past the curve in the trail and away from the pond. Surely, that was far enough. He turned to be certain he wasn't being followed. What met his eyes was impossible. "Oh jeez, how can that be?" he coughed, in shock. The two dogs had not moved; they were both sitting in their puddles on the trail, beside the pond, the same distance from Jason as before. It was as if he had not run at all.

"No, no, no...," he said, beginning to pass into uncontrolled panic, his head shaking back and forth in disbelief. Now, there were four little, black, evil and diseased dogs. Again he turned and ran. But now he was completely out of control; he ran as fast as he could, as there was nothing else he could do. There was no thinking, there was no planning; no further awareness of anything around him, just the intense need to get away, to run!

Pain began to overcome his brain. His legs ached, his lungs gasped for breath, but could not take in enough air. His chest began to hurt, his head began to throb, and he started to get tunnel vision, yet he dare not stop. He forced himself to keep going, but he began to lose control of his legs. He stumbled forward several more yards, lurching, one foot in front of the other, falling forward, trying to catch himself, finally collapsing face first to the ground!. He rolled over onto his back, looking up at the sky through the tree-tops, gasping, his arms and legs spread wide.

After a few seconds, Jason raised his head to look in the direction he had come. They were still there, sitting in their puddles, blindly staring at him through their pure-white, sightless eyes! But now there were six! He had run nearly to death to escape them, but had not moved an inch! The dogs were exactly where they had been when he started to run; sitting in their puddles on the trail, along the edge of the pond. How could that be? What was happening? How could this be happening? Was he going mad?

Suddenly, as Jason watched, all six, little, black diseased dogs stood as one. Without a bark, without any sound at all, they came at him, and they came incredibly fast. It wasn't as if they ran, but rather, it was as though they…projected themselves…across the distance to where Jason lay. They were instantly on him, all over him. He kicked and swung his fists at them, eyes closed, screaming. He rolled one way, then the other, but he could not get away.

He could feel them on him, moving about very quickly, biting and snapping. They were soaking wet and ice-cold, and as he struggled, he felt himself getting wet and very cold. Soon, with the cold and dampness, with the drain of the energy he had expended in trying to get away, and the energy he now expended fighting them, his strength began to fade. He began to mentally go numb; his first step in surrendering life.

In resignation, all will power fading, he rolled onto his side and curled into a fetal position. Just before blacking-out, he opened his eyes. Right in front of him stood the little, black, evil, diseased dog, its oversized head inches from his face, white, sightless eyes staring, mouth full of long, uneven, needle-sharp teeth dripping with blood-stained saliva. It lunged, and Jason screamed!

• • •

"Aaaaaaahhhh!"he moaned, suddenly bolting upright in bed, arms flailing, feet kicking, eyes closed!

Marsha now sat up too, awakened by Jason's sudden movements.

"Jason…Jason…Jason!" yelled Marsha, "Jason, wake up! Wake up, Jason! You're dreaming! Jason! Wake-up, Jason!!" She reached over and grabbed his arms. "Jason…!" she shook him.

He stopped flailing, slowly calmed down, and opened his eyes. "Oh," he groaned. "Oh, my dear God," he said in a low voice. He folded his legs to his chest, wrapped his arms around them, and laid his head down on his knees.

"…you okay?" asked Marsha.

"Yeah, I guess so…" he replied, not looking up.

"You have got to see someone about these dreams; this is getting scary!"

Jason nodded without looking up. "What time is it?"

"Almost five," said Marsha.

"Jeez, I'm soaked with sweat." He sat quiet for a moment. "I think I'll get a shower and go downstairs for coffee…it's a cinch I'm not going back to sleep."

"I'm not getting up yet, okay?"

"Sure, I'll have your coffee ready when you come down."

"Thanks," said Marsha, rolling over and pulling the covers back over her shoulders.

He went down to the kitchen and turned on the coffee maker; the coffee would be ready when he finished his shower. Going quietly back up to the bathroom, he turned on the hot water in the shower, took off his sweat-soaked pjs, threw them into the clothes hamper, and stepped into the wonderful, soothing hot rain of the shower.

He leaned against the shower wall and let the hot water run over his head for a long time before soaping up. Then he rinsed off, turning off the shower. Drying off, he thought, "She's right, this is getting scary." It seemed the dreams were getting worse; what the hell was wrong with him? He quietly went down the steps into the kitchen. As planned, coffee was ready. He took his favorite mug from the cupboard, poured in the coffee, and took a sip. "Wow, that's good," he thought.

The cell-phone charger was plugged in next to the coffee maker. Both his and Marsha's phones were lying on it. He picked his phone up with his right hand and, with his coffee in his left hand, he casually turned away from the coffee maker and leaned back against the kitchen counter.

He pressed the power button on the phone and was surprised to see a voicemail registered on the screen. More surprising, the voicemail was listed as being recorded within the last two minutes. "Odd, the phone didn't buzz or vibrate for the call." he thought. Thumbing his security code into the phone, and activating the phone app icon, he looked for a recent phone number or name. There was nothing, just the record of a voicemail. That was weird. Jason touched the recorded voicemail and put the phone to his ear.

"Heh, heh, heh...!" the rasping, sigh-like voice rushed from the phone through his ear and deep into his brain. His eyes shot open and he recoiled from the sound, throwing his arms up and away; projecting the cell phone across the room and against the opposite wall. The mug of coffee fell from his other hand and shattered onto the kitchen floor. His legs became weak with the terror that consumed him and he slowly slid down the face of the cupboard doors to the floor.

"Oh God, Oh God, Oh God!" he murmured in total terror!

In that instant, he felt his right hand, the one that had held the phone, grow incredibly icy cold and, instinctively, he jerked it up to in front of his eyes. It was dripping wet. Slipping down his hand, then down his little finger, to finally drip to the floor was a filmy, mucus, blood-red-stained string of saliva.

Jason Daniel Edmonton screamed, and he screamed, and he screamed!

4

"The Facilitator"

fiction

*"His visit complete, his purpose fulfilled,
the Facilitator moved on."*

He observed the countenance in the floor length mirror in front of him. A man of average height and of average weight stood looking back. The man had short, strikingly pure white hair. His face was well proportioned and arranged in the pleasant visage of an average Caucasian male. The nose was of average length and width, the corners of the mouth aligned perfectly with the width of the eyes, which were set an average distance apart. They were grey in color with dark brown eye lashes and brows.

The chin was perfectly proportioned to the length of the mouth and the length of the face. The skin was not tanned, nor was it pale, and there were absolutely no blemishes nor was a single hair out of place.

He wore a perfectly tailored black, silk business suit with a matching black silk tie. His shirt, too, was black rather than white, and around his neck hung a 24 karat gold chain. Hanging from the chain at a length to place it directly over the heart, was an overly large 24 karat gold Roman cross. In his left lapel button hole was a 24 karat pin, a perfect match to the cross hanging from the chain, but much smaller.

There seemed to be no discernible expression on his face; no tell-tale laugh lines, no upturn to the corners of his mouth. Neither brow was elevated slightly higher than the other, no twinkle of light glistened from his eyes. His expression was completely neutral, nearly lifeless. Indeed, as his face revealed no emotional expression whatever, so neither did he feel any emotion as he beheld himself in the mirror. There was no feeling of vain pride for the perfection of the manifestation before him. Nor did he feel a need to make any adjustments to the apparition. It was perfect; it fulfilled his purpose.

The mirrored image was not his true form, nor could it be. In his purpose, he could not exhibit his true form; to do so would be...distressful, disconcerting, incomprehensible? How does one describe that which is unimaginable? As he was not biological, he was without gender; all descriptive pronouns applied: he, she, they...it. He was "He" at this time as it applied to his purpose.

He could communicate in every dialect of every human tongue; fluent in languages long latent or forgotten. His depth of knowledge and understanding was complete cognizant comprehension; he knew all that which he knew, and he knew all that which he did not know. He could comprehend the patterned movement of particles infinitesimally smaller than the quark and simultaneously realize their interrelationship with the movements of galaxies yet undiscovered by men. To him, a quasar was as the blossoming of a flower; the singularity of a black hole represented the life potential of a burgeoning seed.

Quantum physics was to him as simple as the addition of whole numbers, and time held no relevance. He was as comfortable in the eleventh century as he was in the twenty-first. He often traveled within each and in all times between, as well as before and after. He was a presence at ten thousand different locations within ten thousand different times and then ten thousand more. Known in literature, mythology, and all religions by many names, he was, is, and forever will be, The Facilitator.

• • •

He walked into the state office building, passing quietly across the marbled floor, no sound audible from His perfectly shined, black patent-leather shoes while the clashing, echoing noise of all those around him bounced from walls to dome to floor. His steps were directed toward the security check point that separated the public area of the building from the offices of the many elected state representatives as well as the offices of the Governor.

At a reception desk near the entrance of security sat a uniformed State Capitol Police Officer, checking appointments and IDs. As He approached, the officer looked up. He smiled at the officer, Samuel Bethany, a black man, age forty-three. Samuel had a wonderful, vivacious wife; a nurse, and three children; two girls and a boy. The Facilitator knew of His coming visit with Samuel. He knew of His coming visits with Samuel's wife and with each of his children. He knew of the circumstances surrounding those coming visits. He knew the times and the dates of those visits and of His purpose in those visits and how He was to facilitate them. His visit with Samuel would be different from His present purpose. His visit with Samuel would be quiet; Samuel would not be aware of His presence. Samuel was a good man. The Facilitator passed by Samuel without challenge.

He passed through the entire security check-point without incident, merely walking through. No one stopped Him, no one questioned Him; almost as though they did not even see Him. Yet, He permitted Himself to be seen. He walked on down a long hall that ended at a bank of elevators. Stopping in front of the first elevator, the door immediately opened without His pressing the call button. He stepped in and turned to the door which immediately closed and the car ascended instantly to the fourth floor: the offices of the Governor.

The outer office was a labyrinth of cubicles and glassed-in side offices, all bustling with staffers in stylish dresses or casual slacks, dress shirts with the sleeves rolled, and loose ties. All were busy on telephones, or focused on computer screens. In several of the side offices, other staff were engaged in conversation around desks or tables, referencing what seemed to be reams of notes. The Facilitator knew each one by name, by thought, by action, and by need; as though they were the leaves of a tree in their millions, yet each single leaf with its own cellular structure; its own vascular system, with its own photosynthetic process, and each enfolding its own intimacy with the tree.

At the opposite end of the outer office was a very large pair of ornate double doors, made of mahogany. On each door was a relief of the great seal of state. In gold lettering, centered above the doors, was a sign that read, "Office of the Governor." He walked easily and slowly across the center of the outer office toward the great doors. Again, He was not questioned nor interfered with, though several staffers sitting near His passage did look up at Him as He walked by. In times to come, when recalling the events of this day, which would come to stand out in the memories of them all, not one would remember a stranger with pure white hair wearing a beautiful black silk suit visiting the offices that day.

Bernice Richards sat at a large, very impressive dark wooden desk opposite the double doors within the inner reception office of the Governor. Her office was large and opulent. Heavy carpeting in a pattern mimicking a classic Persian design of deep reds, blues, and tans covered the entire floor. The walls were papered in beige with a heavy tapestried relief. The high ceiling was framed with dark, heavy crown molding. The north side of the office was a series of floor to ceiling windows, offering a picturesque view of the city. The windows were hung with patterned brocade drapes matching the carpeting and gathered at regular intervals with heavy golden ropes.

On each wall were original works of art borrowed from the state's fine arts museum. Each painting was framed in gold gilt with brass labels at the bottom center, listing the work and the name of the artist. He had visited each one of the artists, in their turn. Around the room, arranged under the paintings, were settees and overstuffed chairs, coffee tables, and end tables with table lamps and various selections of magazines. String music softly filtered throughout the room from speakers imbedded in the ceiling; modern classical pieces from the cello of the great Yo-Yo Ma; Bernice's favorite artist. Bernice's desk sat directly to the left of another large pair of mahogany doors that obviously led to the private office of the Governor.

The Governor had planned a meeting to occur within the next half hour to discuss federal funding that was coming to the state as designated from a bill that had passed Congress the day before. The funding was earmarked for developing infrastructure: highways, bridges, renewed gas and water lines. Sitting around the room were very important men, wearing very expensive suits, who would decide, along with the Governor, where that money would be spent. These very important men were about to decide which contractors were about to become very rich. He knew each man in the room well. Several were facing visits in their futures that would not be pleasant for them. Not one looked up as He entered the room.

Of course, Bernice noticed His entry; Bernice noticed absolutely everything within her realm of responsibility, and within the responsibility of her realm. She was the Administrative Secretary to the Governor. If there was a question in anyone's mind, the long wooden, triangular title plate sitting central, front on her desk was certain to dispel that question. Bernice had worked for the last four governors; this one was her fifth. She had been "Administrative Secretary" to the last three. She knew her job well; she knew the level of power and influence she wielded and she reveled in it. She made absolutely certain that she was indispensable to the governor, for therein lay her power. Every one of the underling staffers in the outer office owed their patronage to her; she held their jobs and their careers in her hands. Make no mistake, these were her offices. This was her life.

Bernice was fifty-seven years old and no longer married. Years ago, when she still had stars in her eyes and still believed in changing the world for the better through politics, she had fallen madly in love with an adviser to the then governor. He was ten years older than she and no longer had any illusions about the game of politics. He was into life for himself alone, both for gain and pleasure. He cheated on her openly, laughing at her pain and her foolish idealism. After seven years, she finally got out.

Three things came out of that relationship for Bernice: a little girl, the loss of the stars in her eyes, and a very handsome settlement. She may have been idealistic but she was not stupid; she kept notes and had pictures. She took him for nearly everything.

The tragedy for Bernice was the loss of the stars in her eyes, as her life became deeply darkened by cynicism and fatalism. Her daughter turned away from her over time because her mother was the most unhappy, cold, and angry person she knew and she didn't want that in her life. Bernice focused on her job, her career, and hid from the rest of the world.

She noticed Him come into the room, of course. But, inexplicably, she let Him pass by her without a word; very unlike her; very unprofessional of her. She had never done such a thing like that before. She even watched Him pass by, and said nothing. She even chided herself inside for her mistake, but said nothing. She even watched Him pass through the heavy wooden doors that separated her office from the Governor's, but made no sound. And, of course, when questioned extensively during the following investigation, like those in the outer office, she would have no recollection of any white-haired stranger in a black suit entering her office that day. If He were capable of compassion, He would have felt it for Bernice. She had missed her life, and as He knew, she had little left.

. . .

Governor William Howard Stratton was deeply engrossed in the list of figures in front of him. These were the particulars of the federal funding coming to the state for infrastructure. He was preparing for the meeting that would happen too quickly. He needed to be prepared, but these numbers had not come through until an hour ago. He probably should reschedule the meeting so he would have more time to prep, but he was excited to get things underway, and he thought to delay the meeting might make him appear even more unprepared. He was beginning to get a handle on things.

He would be fine; he could bull-shit through anything he was unsure of. That had always worked for him before. Also, to delay the meeting would really screw up his schedule. The fall campaign for re-election would need to begin soon. Things were really amping-up with the State Democratic Party. The sooner he got things rolling with this funding, the sooner the positive political impact for his campaign as the voters would begin to see the results of these billions of dollars manifested in concrete construction. No problem, let's get the meeting underway. What the hell is this?

"Hello! Hello! Uh, can I help you sir? How did you find your way into this office? Ha, ha!" Governor Stratton said, in a bit of shock, looking up to see a man standing directly in front of his desk. He tried to stand, but found he could not. Odd! "I'm sorry, sir, did Bernice, my secretary, let you in? I certainly didn't hear her call...must have missed that. Humph..." He looked the man up and down. He was certainly well dressed. He certainly seemed pleasant enough, didn't seem to be offering any kind of threat. Still, how did he get in here?

He stood directly in front of the Governor, looking slightly down at the man sitting across the large, heavy oak desk from Him. His stance placed His feet apart at shoulder width, equal weight on each. He let His arms cross at the wrists evenly, just below the base of the golden cross hanging from the chain around His neck. He looked, unblinkingly, yet not staring, directly into the eyes of the most powerful political figure in the state, a state of over fourteen million inhabitants. He would not move His eyes from the eyes of the Governor throughout the visit.

"I'm sorry sir; you really should not be here. I would be very glad to help you find who you are looking for. You didn't say who you are. What's your name, sir? How can I help you?" The Governor stopped talking. He stared at the white haired man for an awkward moment. After an all too long pause without any answers to his questions, without any word from the man at all, he now began to feel an odd, deep unusual feeling of concern. He found himself staring at the stranger, almost unable to look away, with a deeper feeling of loss of control; a feeling very foreign to him.

Then, from the Man, and seemingly, without any movement of his mouth or lips, came a whisper, low and raspy, yet with an audible power that left no doubt that He had spoken. The words were few, and they passed quickly, but there was no mistaking them; they were succinct and discernible. And they need not, would not, be repeated.

"I am the Facilitator. YHWH wishes to meet with you."

The Governor continued to stare. That was it? That was all? After another long pause, the Governor asked, "I'm sorry, what? I think you said that you are the Facilitator and that Yahweh wishes to speak with me?"

The Man said nothing but continued to stand, unmoving, eyes unblinking, looking at the Governor.

Stratton reached for his office phone. "Bernice, would you please have someone from security come to my office right away. Thank you." (During the subsequent investigation, no record of this call would be found.) He replaced the receiver and looked up at the Facilitator. "Okay, that's enough. Who are you? What are you doing? What do you want? Who is this Yahweh person? Why does he want to meet with me? Now, you have got a lot of questions to answer and little time. I'm extremely busy. Security will be here any moment and unless you start answering some questions, you're going to be in a lot of trouble. So…What?"

The Man continued to look at, through him, unmoving, without any sign of emotion or expression on his face.

The governor now noticed the large gold cross on the chest of his uninvited guest. "Ah, a man of the church," he observed. Then recalling a recent meeting with Bishop O'Neill, he began to smile and chuckle. He pointed to the man before him and began to laugh, "Okay, I get it now. Hahaha! Bishop O'Neill put you up to this, didn't he? He said last week at the dedication luncheon for the new rectory that he would 'get me' for my roasting him in my speech!" He put his head back and let out a good laugh. "…but I figured him out. Didn't I? Huh? I get it! He sent you here to punk me, didn't he? Huh?! It was a good one, but I caught him, huh? Look, the joke is over. A good one! Give the good bishop my regards. He is a great man. Tell him I love him and I got a good laugh!"

The governor opened his desk drawer and pulled out some cash. "Look, you did a great job. Here is some money for lunch. Let me buy you lunch for your trouble. I'd take you to lunch myself, but I have this big meeting, so I can't leave, but let me, at least, buy your lunch for your trouble, okay?"

The Man continued to look at, through him, unmoving, without any sign of emotion or expression on His face.

"Oh, come on now. Here, take the money. It was a good joke; you did your part well. You actually had me there! Ha, Ha! The least I can do is buy your lunch. It's no trouble for me and you won't be committing some great sin by letting the Governor give you money for lunch," Governor Stratton continued, becoming more exasperated at the Facilitator's lack of response. He leaned over the desk and extended the cash toward his visitor.

The Man continued to look at, through him, unmoving, without any sign of emotion or expression on His face.

"Oh here!" Stratton exclaimed, and, being unable to stand, he lunged his body forward over the desk toward his visitor and pushed his arm and hand into the chest of the Facilitator with the intention of forcing the money, and his will, upon this intruder; an intention with which he was most familiar and successful. His hand reached and penetrated the chest of the Facilitator; hand and money passing through the large golden cross, through the black silk shirt, and into what should have been the flesh and bone of the Man. There was no resistance, no impact against the metal of the cross, no wrinkling of the silk shirt, no soft, warm resistance of the Man's skin and muscle, no hard stop against the bone of His sternum; no feeling whatsoever, and no reaction from the Facilitator at all.

For half a second, the Governor sat in unbelieving shock, looking at his hand penetrating within the chest of the Man standing before him, not comprehending what had just occurred. Then Stratton recoiled with a spontaneous, uncontrolled scream, his torso crashing back against his chair, nearly tipping it over backwards. His arm with the hand that had just seemed to impale the Man across the desk from him jerked high above the governor's head, the proffered money fluttering in all directions. Stratton's face turned white, his mouth was agape, and his eyes open wide.

After another few seconds of trying to process the event, he instinctively brought his arm down and looked at his hand, which felt unusually chilled. He looked again at the stranger in front of him, then, in a choking whisper, "Who…what…uhhh…?" He sat for a moment, staring at the Facilitator, and tried again in a chocking whisper, "Who are you? Wha…What just happened? What on Earth is going on here?"

The Facilitator and the Governor remained in place for several minutes; unmoving statues facing one another; a vignette of a projected purpose and an awakening comprehension of cold terror.

The Facilitator continued to look at, through the Governor without any sign or expression on His face; His message had been delivered.

The Governor continued to stare at the Facilitator, blood beginning to return to his face, his expression of shock fading, morphing into an expression of uncertainty and fear as understanding began to dawn in his mind. "No," he finally said quietly. "No…no…no. This can't be happening. Is this how it happens? No…no." He began to shake his head, "No, no, no!"

The Facilitator continued to look at, though him, unmoving, no sign of emotion or expression on his face.

Bill Stratton contemplated his visitor. "This is real, isn't it?" he whispered. He sat staring at the Man. Then his face began to grow red, his eyes became watery, his lips began to quiver. "I've been a good man…a good public servant. I have done my best to serve the people of this state. I am not a corrupt politician…I haven't done anything wrong." Tears began to run down his face as he pleaded, his voice faltering. "I haven't done anything wrong…I…I'm a good man!" He stopped for a second, then, "Oh my god! What about my wife and kids? They're so young… I haven't done anything wrong…why is this happening to me now?" His body began to tremble slightly.

He stopped and sat for a moment. Involuntarily, his right hand came up and covered his mouth. He looked up into the face of the Facilitator, "This is about that girl, isn't it?" he asked quietly through his hand. He continued to stare at the Facilitator for a long moment, then put both his hands over his face. He began to sob and his body shuddered, "I am so sorry! I am so sorry! I never meant for anybody to get hurt! I am so sorry!" He continued to sob.

Lowering his arms, he crossed them on the desktop in front of him and hid his face in them. "I drank too much! It was a boat party celebrating my election. It was on the yacht of one of my biggest donors. I was drunk, she was cute…too young. I didn't know she was too young. I was drunk. I took her to one of the cabins."

He sat up again, looking at his visitor; he spread his arms wide. "I just thought we would talk, but…but, well, things got out of hand! I didn't know what I was doing…I drank too much, I was drunk! She fought me, but… I was drunk. I am so sorry. I didn't want to hurt anyone. I lost control. I…I forced her to…!" Again, he hid his face in his hands.

Bill Stratton dropped his hands to the desktop again and looked forward at nothing, remembering that night four years before. He said nothing for a while, then, "Afterwards, I felt guilty, I felt dirty, horrible, ashamed, filthy. The girl was crying." He paused. "Look, I only wanted to help her, try to make it right with her…you know?"

The Governor's face was cold and ashen now, as he continued, "I asked the owner of the yacht to 'take care of her.' I meant he should give her money and send her home, or to the hospital, to make sure she wasn't hurt, you know?" He looked up at the Facilitator. "He thought I meant that he should 'take care of her,' you know? …Like…make her not be a problem for the Governor; like, make her go away!"

He began to sob again as he faced the tragedy of his actions. "He, he had his people get rid of her. They gave her drugs, lots of drugs; I don't know what they were. Then, they wrapped her in a tarp with some weights, and dropped her in the ocean." There was a long pause. "I guess they thought she would be an embarrassment to me, would call me out, cause a scandal, destroy my career, I don't know." Again, he paused, "I didn't know what I was doing… I was drunk! I am so very sorry!" Governor William Howard Stratton continued to stare at nothing, his face grey and tear-streaked. He was quiet for some time, then said very quietly, "I didn't try to stop them." A moment later, "I didn't even know her name…"

The time had come. He finally began to look away from the sad, tragic, deflated human in front of him; this most powerful man of the state; this lost soul with promised, yet worthless, billions of dollars lying on the desk before him. The Governor noticed the Man begin to move and to turn away. Terror now flooded his senses, "Where are you going?" he whispered hoarsely. So recently concerned at His unexpected appearance, the Governor was now terrified at the finality of His departure. "Don't leave! Stay! Help me! Please, don't leave!" Tears running down his face, he begged the Facilitator, "What happens now…what happens to me now? Where do I go? Help Me! Please don't leave…please…don't leave!"

His visit was concluded, His purpose fulfilled. What was now to happen to the Governor was not in His purpose. What was to happen to Governor Bill Stratton, and where he was to go, were not of His concern. Those decisions were for another meeting, to be made by One of far greater power. He had no further interest; He had other visits to make; other meetings to facilitate. He turned away from the lost man without hesitation and moved toward the large, mahogany doors leading back into Bernice Richard's office.

As He passed through the doors, the visage of the man Bernice and Governor Stratton had seen began to fade. As He passed Bernice's desk, the form He had taken disintegrated into the billions of disparate elemental atoms that had comprised the former, mortal structure. As the clouded vision passed by Bernice's desk, a chilled breath from the swirling atomization dispersal of the apparition pushed several papers up and away from the surface of the desk. Bernice felt the chill and tried, unsuccessfully, to grab the papers.

"What the hell was that?" she asked herself, looking around disconcertedly. Finding no answer to her question, she shrugged, then stood and retrieved the papers which now lay about the floor in front of the desk. She straightened them and put them where she had placed them before. She looked at her watch; it was past time for the planned meeting. She went around the desk and picked up the phone receiver and punched the Governor's line. She waited, there was no reply. "Sir? Governor?"

Odd, she thought; she knew he was in there; he would never leave his office without informing her. She replaced the receiver and went to the doors and knocked. No answer. She knocked again and quietly opened the door and looked in. Seeing the back of the governor's head above the back of his chair, which was turned away from her, she confidently opened the door and went in.

A moment later, the important men looking at their watches with irritation; waiting impatiently on the planned meeting in which they would make other men rich, and gain great favor for their efforts in return, jumped at Bernice's ear-piercing scream from within the Governor's office.

There would be no meeting this day, or for some time to come. The Governor's schedule had changed; he was destined for another, more pressing meeting; a meeting that takes precedence above all others.

His visit completed, His purpose fulfilled, the Facilitator moved on.

5

"Billy"
fiction

"Billy, I choose to live in the Sun."

The old wood frame house stood on the lower talus slope of a hill overlooking Spring Valley Road, about two and a half miles south of the village of Scenery Hill, Pennsylvania. It was typical of an early twentieth century "company house" built throughout coal country, USA: Western Pennsylvania, West Virginia, Southern Ohio, and Eastern Kentucky. Uncharacteristically, it stood alone, rather than in a row of carbon copy houses in a "coal patch." Characteristically, it exhibited the careworn, faded dilapidation and depression so common to its kind. It had been white at one time, but was now a faded grey. Weeds grew around the foundation and the bushes bordering the front steps were long past pruning. The front porch railing was missing stanchions, giving it the appearance of the Cheshire Cat in need of dental work.

It was a narrow two-story with a simple gable roof, front to back. There was a covered porch on the front and a lean-to, shed-style addition on the back, for storage. Through the front door was the front room, or living room, with an open stairway to the second floor on the left. Behind the front room was a combination kitchen, eating room, with a back door leading through the storage area, outside, to the privy. The unused privy to this house still stood, abandoned, ignored, unpainted, and canting to one side, surrounded by weeds. Sometime in the past, a small bathroom was added to the house by sectioning-off part of the kitchen, eating area and installing a septic system.

The stairway to the second floor was open with a simple, utilitarian railing. At the top of the stairs was the largest of the three bedrooms. A hallway parallel with the steps led to the other two, smaller bedrooms.

A gravel driveway led sharply up the talus slope from the road to level off along the west side of the house, then around to the back where it faded into the crab grass and dandelions of the back yard. There was no garage. An old rusty metal shed stood toward the end of the back yard and protected an ancient push mower and attendant red plastic two-gallon jug of gasoline. A battered, sixteen foot aluminum canoe lay up against the shed, turned upside down to prevent it filling with rain water. Sitting in the driveway was an old Chevy pickup truck, vintage 1984. It was black, coated with coal dust, its fenders and doorsills rusting out, the windshield cracked, and the tires nearly bald. A matching spare was thrown into the bed.

A fairly new and well-built ramp of treated lumber inclined up from the edge of the driveway to the level of the back door of the lean-to addition at the rear of the house where it joined an eight foot by six foot deck of the same material. The well-built ramp and deck contrasted starkly against the condition of the house it served and told its own story of trials, tribulations, and neighborly kindness.

Within the front room stood a heavy metal hospital bed with its attachments of cranks, springs, and bar lifts. The mattress was bare as were the three pillows, obviously used at one time for additional support and elevation. Beside the bed stood a folded wheel chair, and a walker with a homemade, quilted bag still hung from its front bar, stuffed with personal accoutrements. A hospital-style, adjustable, rolling service table sat against the wall near the bottom of the bed.

At one end of the front porch hung a wooden porch swing, unpainted, its chains and springs showing a dusting of rust. At the opposite end of the porch stood an old-fashioned, drop-leaf, wooden kitchen table with a matching wooden kitchen chair at one end. On the table was an assortment of potted plants in a group of ceramic and plastic pots in a myriad array of sizes and colors. Several beer cans, soda cans, and empty plates accompanied the green plants in their circus of containers.

The remainder of the porch furnishings consisted of two well-worn aluminum and woven vinyl strap lawn chairs. One of the green and white vinyl straps on one of the chairs was torn and hanging down under the seat, making the chair of questionable use.

Sitting in the other lawn chair, just to the side of the front door, was William Henry Morgan the Third. He was dressed in an old, white t-shirt with the sleeves cut away and a pair of naturally faded blue jeans with a hole in the left knee and frayed at the ankles. Patrons of high end Manhattan clothing stores would pay over one hundred dollars for those jeans. William Henry Morgan the Third paid twelve-fifty at K-Mart in Washington, PA. They had been the blue-light special of the day.

William Henry Morgan the Third kept his brown hair short, had brown eyes to match, and was of medium height of five foot, eight inches. He was well toned and muscular for his age, weighing one hundred and seventy pounds. He sported a beard, in need of a trim, that was mostly brown but turning white at the temples and directly under his chin. In his right hand was a can of Budweiser; in his left hand a burning Marlboro cigarette, the ashes of which he absently flicked onto the porch. He wore no shoes or socks and around his feet lay half a dozen "dead soldiers," empty Bud cans among the cigarette ashes. Just away from his left foot, well within easy reach, was an opened cardboard case of

Budweiser. In the breast pocket of his t-shirt was an open pack of Marlboros. There were more of both in the kitchen. William Henry Morgan the Third was forty-five years old. William Henry Morgan the Third would never be forty-six.

"Billy," what everyone called him, was a coal miner like his father, William Henry Morgan the Second, and his grandfather, William Henry Morgan the First. His grandfather first bought the property in 1922. His great-grand father came to America in 1895 from Wales. He, too, had been a coal miner, in both the old country and the new. The Morgans were Welsh, and coal dust ran in the blood of the Welsh. When Billy's great-grandfather heard of the wonderful opportunities of the growing coal business in America, he had to look for the better life. After all, in America, the streets were paved with gold. Or, at least for Great-Grandfather Morgan, they were paved with coal.

So Billy's great-grandfather died in a coal mine accident in Pennsylvania instead of in Wales. His grandfather died from working in the coal mines, causes unknown. His father died too young, at sixty-two, from working in the coal mines, causes known; a heart attack brought on by excessive smoking and COPD. And now, it was Billy's turn.

It was true, they had chosen their lifestyle, and it was a rugged one. They smoked and they drank, liberally and heavily. All the Morgans were known in the bars and taverns of Brownsville and Washington. Mining was hard, rough, a dirty and dangerous job, with its accompanying hard, rough, dirty, and deadly sins. It was what they did; it was what they had always done. Billy's life mantra was, "Life's a bitch, then you die." It was an easy thing to say on your fourth beer with your buddies, in a bar in Brownsville. Not so easy when looking death in the face.

• • •

Billy had led the typical life of a miner's son in Appalachia. He attended grade school with less than stellar, but passing, grades. That was fine; he was going into the mines, not the halls of Harvard. High school was the same; passing grades and the requisite successful career on the gridiron, with the after-game partying while coaches and parents looked the other way. Four years passed, followed by graduation in 1965, followed by a descending crew elevator into the bowels of the Earth.

But for Billy, things were different. William Henry Morgan the Second, his father, had learned to hunt and fish from his father. He had learned the ways of the woods and he had learned the forests of north-central Pennsylvania. He respected the land; its flora and fauna, and he loved hunting and fishing. He loved hiking and spending time among the trees and did his best to see that his son learned to love all that as well.

Nearly every summer and fall weekend, beginning with Billy's sixth birthday, was spent in the hills of Allegheny National Forest. Throughout his childhood, Billy learned the ways of woodcraft. He learned to hunt various game and how to handle different firearms. His father could not afford a fishing boat, but the lakes, rivers, and streams of Pennsylvania were not strangers to the canoe, and Billy learned to master the delicate craft as well as any early American Indian. Too, William Henry Morgan the

Second could not afford a fancy camper, but he could afford a tent, and sleeping bags, camp chairs, and a cooler.

Billy's mother, Florence, had no interest in hunting and fishing, but she enjoyed being where her husband was, and she did enjoy the outdoors and hiking. Many weekends, the family went together into the woods up north, around Marienville, Kane, and along Tionesta Creek. They immersed themselves in the quiet of the woods, the colors of the autumn leaves, the crisp air of fall, the sounds of the many falls along the streams, and the warmth and camaraderie of the evening campfire.

In the late fall, Billy and his father would spend a week deer hunting at their camp near Allegheny Reservoir, close to the New York State line. Billy's grandfather bought the camp many years earlier. It was small, a shack really, a wood frame building with no insulation, indoor plumbing, or central heat. There was an old, cast-iron, wood burning stove which more than kept the shack warm as long as the fire was tended. The camp sat along a logging road that was maintained by McKean County. For Billy and his father, it was almost heaven.

The camp was furnished with two bunks, a table and chairs. There were shelves and a metal dry sink by one of the windows, and plenty of counter space. Outside the shack, the camp encompassed only about one-quarter acre of land. Billy's father kept plenty of firewood stacked behind the shack. There was an outside fire ring and a tall tepee-like frame of three poles used to dress-out deer they might take during their week at the camp. Mrs. Morgan detested the dirty shack, and was more than happy to leave it to her husband and son.

Among Billy's most cherished memories were those trips to the camp during deer season. He really didn't care about taking a deer, but he loved the evening fire; watching the dancing flames while his dad told him stories of bear hunting or of catching the really big ones along the Clarion River. His back would be freezing while his legs, knees, and face would be roasting. He'd have to stand up and turn around periodically to warm his butt. And the two of them would laugh as Billy had to move his chair to keep out of the smoke that seemed to follow him around the fire's outer circumference.

Mornings were the best. He would wake up to the sound of his father getting out of his bunk and stamping on his boots to go out for more firewood. Billy would lie on his back and watch his breath condense in the cold air above his face while he was snug and warm in his sleeping bag. It was early, usually before five in the morning and long before the sun was up. He would watch his father light the old Coleman lantern he kept at the camp, then start the fire in the stove and put the coffee pot on top to get water boiling.

Billy would get up then and get dressed. They would work together to make breakfast; eggs, bacon, biscuits, sliced potatoes with onion, and coffee. His father made the coffee the old fashioned way by putting a measure of grounds directly into the boiling water, letting the grounds steep for several minutes, then pour in cold water to cause the floating grounds to settle to the bottom of the pot. It was the best coffee in the world!

Billy's childhood and adolescent years were filled with school, a simple family life, weekend trips into the woods, football, and the beginnings of his career underground. It seemed a life worth living and, for Billy, there seemed few cares.

He did have the scare of the possibility of going to war right after graduation. The nation was in the agony of the Vietnam War, and Billy was listed 1-A by the local draft board. Truthfully, his father was worried far more than he was, and his mother was terrified. Billy was pretty laid back and thought that if he had to go, well, it would be okay, a new adventure. As it turned out, he failed the physical with a heart murmur from birth.

William Henry Morgan and his son became a well-known father-son team at Hannon Coal, Mine #2 over the next several years. They began each day with a heavy breakfast prepared by a doting Florence, then drove together in his father's pick-up the twelve miles of county roads to the mine. After eight hours in the dark, they emerged from the shaft and went straight to the "shower shack" provided by the company after the last contract negotiations. When they arrived home, they were clean and ready for dinner.

Evenings were spent on the front porch when the weather permitted, or watching TV sitcoms and game shows in the winter. Billy's father and mother particularly liked, "All in the Family," possibly because their lives so paralleled those of Archie and Edith. Each day of each week of each month was pretty much the same, until August 12, 1987.

William Henry Morgan the Second got up from the dinner table. He thanked his wife, Florence, for another very fine dinner, and asked his son, Billy, to help Florence clean up. He always told his wife that the dinner was fine, and it always was; he always asked his son to help clean up, which his son always did, because William Henry Morgan the Second was raised that way.

William Henry Morgan the Second also truly loved both his wife and his son. This evening, he walked out of the kitchen, through the living room, pushed open the front screen door, walked across the porch, sat down on the top of the front steps, pulled a pack of cigarettes from his shirt pocket, fell over sideways onto the steps, and died. Like the once-white company row house in which he lived, Billy's life began to fade to grey.

• • •

Florence was never the same after her husband's death. She had never been a strong woman and seemed to always be susceptible to colds and whatever flu virus was prevalent from year to year. Her life had orbited around her husband; she had adored him. His nightly compliments about her dinners were well earned as she poured over recipe and cooking magazines during any spare time she had. Her purpose hung upon his compliments. Although limited in her resources, Florence kept a clean house for William Henry Morgan the Second to come home to. And, she reserved at least one hour each afternoon to prepare herself for his arrival, making certain her hair was just right and her make-up was most attractive without being over the top.

She always wore a dress in the evenings despite her limited wardrobe. With his death, she lost her focus. Over time, the house became less clean and gradually more cluttered. She also lost interest in caring for herself. The nights were more frequent that Billy came home to find his mother still in her nightgown, watching television, with no meal prepared at all. It became common for the wastebaskets to be overflowing while the refrigerator was empty. She became withdrawn and uncommunicative. She would often sit and stare at the TV for hours without saying anything to Billy, and when he tried to talk with her, she didn't seem to hear him.

One evening, a little over a year and a half after his father's death, Billy came home from the mine to find Florence sitting on the kitchen floor in a puddle of her own piss. She was dressed in the same nightgown she had worn for the last two and a half days; her hair hung, unwashed, in matted strings over her face. When Billy tried to talk to her he received no response whatever. He knelt down on one knee and turned her face up so he could see her. Her left eyelid was closed and the right eye seemed to have no focus. The left side of her face drooped grotesquely downward. Billy called the fire department.

The stroke was debilitating. Diagnostic scans indicated a massive bleed into the right side of her brain. Florence was completely paralyzed on her left side. She could not move her left extremities, nor could she talk. She was placed in a nursing home for a period of convalescence and physical therapy. Billy was told to prepare for her care. He had not the slightest idea what that meant. For a single-income coal miner, it meant devastation.

With advice from other miners who had faced health problems over the years and from the social workers at the hospital and the nursing home, Billy was able to establish a tolerable living routine for his mother and himself. He had some money from his father's life insurance and, with that, he was able to buy the needed equipment to take care of his mother at home. There was no way he could afford a nursing facility for her. The living room became her sanctuary. In reality, other than her inability to move around, her life continued as the tragedy it had become even before her stroke.

Supplementing his father's life insurance with his own pay, Billy was able to hire in-home nursing care for Florence while he worked. He spent his evenings and weekends taking care of her. At first, friends and neighbors helped out by bringing food and occasionally caring for Florence on a Saturday evening so he could go out with friends from the mine. They built the deck and ramp onto the house that allowed Billy to wheel his mother to the pickup for doctor appointments and an occasional outing. But, as the new way life settled into routine, interest and aid from friends became rare and Billy's life became solely caring for his mother.

• • •

Billy jerked his left hand back as the burning cigarette butt finally reached his fingers. "Damn it!" he exclaimed, dropping the butt to the porch floor among the dozen or so that already lay there, and shook his burnt fingers. With Billy's sudden movements came a long series of dry wrenching coughs causing him to double over. Now completely awakened from the trance he had fallen into over the last twenty minutes, he took a deep breath, which resulted in more coughing. He looked around himself as if he was just becoming aware of where he was.

Fact was, he had been sitting there since before noon; since he had returned from his appointment with the oncologist in Washington. He got up from the green and white lawn chair, went into the house to the bathroom and peed. Returning to the front porch, Billy walked to the top of the steps and looked out over the hay field on the other side of the road.

"Looks like it's ready for second cutting," he thought absently. He then turned and sat back down in the lawn chair, leaned over, and pulled another "Bud" from the cardboard box by his left foot.

"Shit! What the hell am I gonna do?"

Florence had died three years almost to the day after her husband. It had been a very difficult time for Billy. He had a hard time meeting her needs; she could not talk or communicate beyond pointing with her right hand, or blinking at his request, and she often became confused as to what she was even trying to indicate. She cried a lot, and for no obvious reason. He could never really console her. Although it became routine to help her go to the bathroom, or to bathe her, he never got used to it and was always embarrassed. It was the same getting her to bed each night. Fortunately, she could feed herself with her right hand, after weeks of physical therapy.

Doctor appointments were an ordeal involving a bath, dressing, wheeling her to the truck, lifting her into the truck, and then lifting her out again at the doctor's office. Coming home was everything in reverse but the bath. Sometimes he would take her for a ride after appointments, or take her to get her hair done, or to a restaurant. Restaurants were rare, because money was scarce.

He had to take time off, or vacation, to take Florence to the doctor. The bosses at the mine knew Billy's situation, but their tolerance was limited. Too often he had to take time off without pay, because he had no choice. He had in-home nursing care from six in the morning to five in the afternoon, five days a week. It was very expensive and was draining the savings they had received from his father's life insurance, even with supplementing it from his own pay. He spent many evenings sitting on the porch, long after putting Florence to bed, worrying what was going to happen to them. Tragically, it was fortunate when Florence died; what little money was left was quickly dwindling. It was also fortunate that Billy's father had purchased thirty thousand dollars of life insurance for his wife when he bought his own.

• • •

Billy started coughing sometime just before Florence died. That was not quite two years ago. It wasn't a bad cough and, at first, he paid little attention to it. As the months went by, he began to have coughing spells in the mornings while he was getting ready for work. These happened more often as weeks passed. One particular time, he had a bad coughing spell while driving to the mine. It was so bad, he had to pull over and stop because he couldn't concentrate on the road. He soon forgot about it through the distractions of the day.

The problem intensified with time and with cigarettes; Billy was a three pack a day smoker. People started to notice his coughing spells and his miner buddies would make jokes about it. After some time, they stopped making jokes about it and started asking him if he was all right. "Hey, I'm fine," he'd say, brushing them off. But he wasn't fine. So, when he got scared enough, he went to the doctor.

The doctor asked him questions, listened to his chest, and referred him for x-rays. When the doctor saw the x-rays, he referred Billy for a CT-scan for a closer look and then referred him to a pulmonologist at the hospital in Washington, Pa. The pulmonologist asked Billy some questions, listened to his chest, and looked at Billy's work-up. He then referred Billy to an oncologist in Pittsburgh. Today, Billy had gone to see the oncologist.

"Shit, what the hell am I gonna do?" thought Billy to himself for at least the one-hundredth time as the sun was setting over the hayfield across the road. Still, he didn't have an answer to his question. When he had asked the oncologist the same question, the doctor talked of various medications, chemotherapy regimens, and radiation.

Billy was quickly overcome. His second question for the oncologist was, "Am I going to die?"

"Well, Mr. Morgan, I don't like to discuss life limits with my patients. Of course we are all going to die, someday. But, with the proper treatments, medications, radiation, and chemo, we know we can extend the lives of cancer patients and give them good, quality time. I think we need to set up a routine of chemo treatments and radiation for you at the hospital in Washington. Uh, that's closer and easier for you than coming to Pittsburgh on a regular routine, isn't it?" He looked at Billy expectantly.

Realizing the oncologist expected some kind of answer, Billy nodded his head.

"We'll set up treatments for a month, twice per week, then do another CT and see how you're doing. That sound good for you, Mr. Morgan?" Without waiting for an answer, he went on.

"Now, I'm going to have my nurse call in this medication for you." He was scribbling things on a little printed form. "You stop by the pharmacy on the fourth floor on your way to the parking garage, and they should have it ready for you. It's just something to help you with the bad cough; take it each morning with your breakfast, and evening, before you go to bed. If you feel like you're going to have a severe coughing spell, I'm also going to prescribe an aerosol. You carry that with you, it's just a little canister you can carry in your pocket. But if you feel a bad coughing spell coming on, you just put it close in front of your mouth and spray it into your mouth while you inhale, understand?"

Again, he did not wait for an answer. "Now, you stop at the nursing station on your way out and give these prescriptions to the nurse there and she'll call them in. Also, I'm going to want to see you in a week. By that time, we should have you scheduled for your treatments in Washington. In a week we'll tell you how that works, what to expect, see how you're doing, okay?"

Billy stared at him.

"Mr. Morgan, there is no point in worrying; we are going to take good care of you, Okay? Okay! I'll see you in a week. Follow me and I'll show you where the nursing station is. Oh, do you have a parking ticket? The nurse will stamp that for you and you won't have to pay for parking. Okay, now follow me, Okay?"

Billy stared at the setting sun, but didn't really see it. He went over his experience with the oncologist again. He was supposed to go back next Thursday afternoon. He'd have to take off work, again. Then he'd have to take off work two days a week for a month for treatments, "What's that…eight days? Plus today and next Thursday; ten days, two weeks. Hope I have enough vacation…," Billy thought. "Vacation… Shit, what the hell am I gonna do?" He sat quietly staring for some time. Then, with his eyes tearing at the realization, said out loud, "I'm gonna die…" After a minute of thought, he said, again, aloud, "I'm gonna die…Ha! Life's a bitch, then ya die…Ha!" William Henry Morgan the Third finally fell asleep in the folding lawn chair after finishing off three more 'Buds' and two Marlboros.

• • •

With the rising sun, Billy had his answer: Vacation!

He stood up and stretched, looking across the hay field on the other side of the road. "Yep, 'bout time for second cutting." He went through the front door into the house, passed through the front room, the kitchen, and out onto the deck. He pissed out into the back yard through the railing spindles, then groaned and leaned over the railing and puked up the remains of half a dozen beers.

After taking a long, hot shower in the tiny, less-than-clean bathroom, he put on clean clothes, got into his father's old truck and drove into Washington. His first stop was the bank, where, after some time with the assistant manager, Billy withdrew twenty thousand dollars of his mother's life insurance money. He had planned to save that money for retirement, but that wasn't going to be a problem anymore.

Second stop was the Ford garage, where after some time talking with the assistant sales manager and a regular salesman, Billy bought a brand new, blue, Ford F-150 pickup truck. He haggled a while about the trade-in, but they would not budge. They gave him five hundred dollars for the old truck, and an aluminum bed cap with windows on the side for the new truck. It was a pretty good deal. He paid cash, $13,500, tax, title, and out the door. The truck wasn't top of the line, but it had a radio and air. It was the first new truck William Henry Morgan the Third ever had. It was the first new truck any William Henry Morgan had ever had.

Billy stopped by the K-Mart and bought a cooler, a new flashlight, and some batteries, then went to the supermarket and bought food and ice for the cooler. Then he drove home. He packed the new pickup with camping supplies his mother and dad had left him; a tent, two sleeping bags, one for padding in the bed of the truck, a Coleman lantern and camp stove. He packed a little bag with underwear, t-shirts, an extra pair of blue jeans; socks, his hunting boots, and then he stood back and took stock.

He turned from the truck and looked at the old house with the nice new ramp and deck. Then he went into the kitchen and got what was left of his stock of beer and cigarettes. He put the beer into the cooler, threw the cigarettes onto the seat of the pickup, got into the driver's seat, and headed down the driveway. As he was passing along the house and the front porch, he hit the brakes. He got out of the truck, went up on the porch, and grabbed the one good lawn chair. He threw it into the back of the truck with everything else, then took a beer out of the cooler and popped the tab.

He took a long drink, reached into the cooler again for a second beer, got into the truck, turned right onto the road, and headed up the hill into Scenery Hill. He turned left onto old US Route 40 and headed west toward Interstate 70. He hadn't locked the house. What for? He wasn't coming back. He hadn't even called off work. What for? William Henry Morgan the Third was gonna die. But first, he was gonna live. He had over six thousand dollars in his pocket and was driving a brand new pickup truck. Billy was going to take a vacation.

He stopped at the truck stop at the intersection of Interstate 70 and Pennsylvania 519. After filling-up the truck, he went in and bought a U.S. Highway Atlas, and snacks for the road. He sat in the truck for a while figuring where to go. Interstate 70 went west through Washington, crossed the Ohio River at Wheeling, then on through Columbus, Dayton, Indianapolis, across Illinois, the Mississippi, through St. Louis. "Well," he thought, "Not much to see before St. Louis. Prolly stay somewhere in Illinois overnight tonight, then stop to see the big arch tomorrow." He tossed the atlas aside, took a big swig of beer, pulled out onto the highway and up the ramp onto I-70 west. Quickly getting the new F-150 up to 75mph, Billy got comfortable for the long haul across Ohio and Indiana.

That night he slept in the back of the pickup at a rest stop west of Terra Haute, Indiana. In the morning he made coffee on the camp stove on the tailgate of the pickup. He decided to stop at a McDonalds down the road for breakfast instead of eating out of the cooler. He went into the rest stop and went to the bathroom. There wasn't anyone else in the restroom; it was 5:30 in the morning. After washing his face, he stood and looked at himself for a long time in the mirror. "What're ya doin', Billy?" he asked himself.

Feeling a lonely lost feeling start to settle over him, he slapped himself across the cheek. He instantly regretted it as he bent over in a long series of dry coughs. Holding tightly to the side of the sink, he finally regained control. He took the aerosol from his pocket and inhaled the medication. "Shit," he said loudly. "Can't let it get to me! Dammit! Gotta go! Move on! Yeah!" He took another quick look in the mirror and left the restroom.

Stopping at a Mickey-D's outside of Effingham, Illinois, he ordered two bacon, egg and cheese biscuits, hash browns, and a large orange juice through the drive-thru, then ate in the truck while he looked at the atlas. "Okay, the arch, then where? Big decision!" He turned to the page with the map of the whole USA on it, researching his options for a long-term route. "North it is," he said.

Folding up the atlas, he got out of the truck and threw away his trash, went into the McDonald's restroom and peed, then headed for St. Louis and the Arch.

The setting sun of his second day of vacation found him headed north on I-61, crossing the state line into Iowa. The Arch had been interesting, but really crowded, which he did not like. He rode the tiny car up the inside of the Arch. It was creepy as the car clanked and bumped, changing attitude each time it altered its angle to fit the ascending curve of the Arch. Also, he had to ride up with three strangers; an older man, his wife and their granddaughter. It was awkward and nobody talked, because nobody talks in elevators. Once at the top, it was cool to look out the little windows, straight down, and with nothing under you.

The next day, he drove north through Iowa without stopping except for gas and bathrooms. When he intersected Route 20 in Dubuque, he turned west again heading for Sioux City and Nebraska. He had never seen such flat land and big fields of corn. The corn wasn't quite ready for harvest, but still tall. At one point, as he drove along, he realized that he could see nothing in any direction but the highway ahead of him, tall corn on either side, and blue sky above.

That night, he stayed at a KOA campground so he could get a shower; he was getting pretty ripe. He started a fire and cooked some baked beans, roasted a couple hot dogs and drank a couple beers. Sitting, watching the fire, he realized he had not coughed much during the day. Away from the fire, it was pretty chilly. He decided to sleep with the tailgate open; the cool night air would feel good and his sleeping bag would keep him plenty warm, just like the nights at the camp with his dad. But this time, his dad wasn't here.

In Sioux City, Billy turned north again heading for South Dakota. He would go to Mt. Rushmore, and then head for Montana to see the Little Big Horn Battlefield. He wanted to go to Glacier National Park, and back south to Yellowstone. He was very excited to see the Rocky Mountains; and he was not disappointed. He was awed. He had never seen any mountains bigger than the Alleghenies, back home. He spent three days camping and hiking in Glacier National Park. He was blown away with the geysers in Yellowstone and had never seen anything as beautiful as Grand Prismatic Spring.

Driving south from Yellowstone to Grand Teton, he was again captured by the beauty of the mountains. He decided to stay in a motel in Jackson Hole. Why not, he had the money. The next morning, he enjoyed a real sit-down breakfast in a restaurant, toured the town, and headed for

Jenny Lake. Later, he rented a campsite at the National Park campgrounds. Toward evening, he decided to drive a ways down the Snake River Valley with the "Big Tits" off to his right. He pulled into a parking area to gaze at the mountains awhile and drink a beer. Leaning against the hood of the truck, he heard strange snorting sounds. When he looked over the ledge of the parking lot into the valley, a herd of elk was grazing its way up the valley toward Teton Lake.

Billy was having a good vacation. Well, as good a vacation as he could; he was dying. That was always there, hanging over him like a dark curtain. He was seeing many things he had only imagined before or had seen in picture books in the high school library. Yet, he was getting tired and he had not imagined how lonely he would become during his long drive. He had been gone for ten days and although he had not planned to, he was thinking about returning home.

"Shit! What's there to go back to?" he thought, staring into the fire his last night in the Tetons. "Hell, what I oughta do is just take a long walk into these mountains and get lost. Don't come back…nobody'd prolly ever find me. Shit, nobody'd even know to look." He stirred the fire with his stir-stick. "Maybe a grizzly'd get me. That'd be quick anyway." He laughed without humor, "Life's a bitch, then ya die." Next day, he drove south, headed for Colorado, Rocky Mountain National Park, and Pike's Peak.

Passing along the Front Range, he went through Fort Collins, Boulder, and Denver. He decided to forego Rocky Mountain National Park. He would drive up Pike's Peak, then head for Arizona to see the Grand Canyon, maybe. Then again, maybe he would just turn left; go home. "Hell, maybe give the doctor a chance to fix me; stranger things have happened," he thought.

The drive up Pike's Peak was scarier than he had expected, but worth it. The cold air at the top was exhilarating after the hot air around Denver. He stood at the overlook railing with his eyes to the east. He took a few deep breaths of the mountain air, and then inhaled his aerosol, just in case.

"This is great, but it really sucks by myself," he thought. He stood there for a long time until the chilly, thin air forced him back into his pickup.

The highway east crossed the desert plains of Colorado; the part of the state nobody ever talks about. The highway was good old Interstate 70; the road he'd started on his trip west. He crossed into Kansas in the early evening and looked for a place to stay the night. He found a campground near Colby. Since he was only spending one night, he didn't put up the tent; he would sleep in the bed of the truck. He built a fire and opened a beer, sitting in the green and white lawn chair, and stared into the flames, waiting for them to die down to cooking coals.

While he sat there, an old Dodge van pulled into the camp site next to his. He watched as a tall thin man got out of the van, walked to the back, opened the doors and pulled out a wheel chair. He then went to the sliding door on the passenger side of the van and opened it. Sitting in the seat was a little girl. The man leaned forward, reached-in with both arms, picked her up and put her into the wheel chair. The man wheeled the little girl over to the picnic table that accompanies all campsites everywhere. Then he went back to the van and started to unload equipment: a cooler, a Coleman stove, a couple of sleeping bags, a tent, a camp chair, cooking pots, and so on.

Billy glanced over to where the little girl sat in the wheel chair, looked back to the man, then quickly back to the girl; she was strikingly beautiful. He could only see the right side of her face in silhouette, but she had huge eyes, a perfect nose, and full lips. Her features were in perfect proportions. She had the blackest hair Billy had ever seen, straight, hanging to below her shoulders, with bangs over her forehead. Billy could not see any obvious reason for her being in the wheelchair.

Billy forced himself to look back to the man, who had begun to erect the tent. He was obviously having trouble with it. Billy watched him struggle with the tent for a few minutes, then got-up and walked over, "Can I help you with that?" he offered.

Surprised, the man jumped and turned toward Billy. He laughed, "Ya scared me! Man, I could use some help. I sure do appreciate the offer." Together, they had the tent up in about ten minutes. When it was up the man stood back and looked at it, laughed, and said, "Well, I guess it'll keep the rain off and that's all we need."

He laughed again and turned to Billy, "Thank you so much! Say, my name's Bob Tompkins." He stuck his open hand out to Billy.

"Billy Morgan, nice to meet you." They shook hands.

"I can't thank you enough, Mr. Morgan. I couldn'a done it without cha." He turned toward the little girl, "This is my daughter, Angelica. Say hello to Mr. Morgan, Ang!"

Billy looked to where Angelica sat, and his heart dropped into his stomach. As beautiful as the right side of her face was, the left side was as terribly deformed. The left side of her face was heavily scarred, apparently from burning and scar tissue replacement. The nostril of her nose was nearly gone, and her left eye was out of alignment with the right. Her mouth seemed to be normal, the left side of her lips appearing to be the mirror image of the right side. Naturally Billy was shocked and had to catch himself to not react. He controlled himself and purposely walked over to her and offered his hand, "Hello Angelica. Nice to meet you," he said and smiled.

"Pleased to meet you, Mr. Morgan," came the reply from a smile that was totally counter to the visage before him.

Billy tried not to stare and turned back to Bob Tompkins. "Well, nice to meet you. I better get back to my fire before it goes out. You folks have a nice evening." He walked back to his campsite.

He roasted two bratwurst over the fire, putting American processed sandwich cheese in the buns, then the hot brats, covered with mustard and relish. After eating, he built up the fire and planned a quiet evening watching the flames. He could hear Bob Tompkins and his daughter cooking their dinner on the Coleman stove in the next site and, as the sun was going down, he watched Bob wheel his daughter toward the restrooms to get ready for bed. He could not help but think back on the hundreds of times he had done the same service for his mother. He felt sad about the whole thing. He felt sad he had not done more for his mother. He felt sad for this little girl and whatever tragedy had caused her deformity. "Dammit! Life's a bitch and then you die."

It was after ten when he sensed Mr. Thompkins approaching his fire. He was torn; he planned to leave early in the morning and should go to bed, but at the same time, he was tired of being alone with no one to talk to. "Howdy, neighbor!" came Tompkin's overly cheerful voice.

"Hey! How ya doin?" he replied without looking up.

"Mind if I share your fire? I love a campfire. Angelica is asleep, so I thought I'd drop over."

"Not at all," Billy replied. It was a partial lie.

Tompkins had brought his own chair and placed it strategically to avoid the smoke.

"How ya doin' t'night?" he opened.

"Pretty good, you? Beer?" offered Billy.

"Oh, no. No, thanks. Where ya from?" asked Mr. Tompkins.

"Western PA, south of Pittsburgh."

"Really! That's a long way off! What brings you here?"

The small talk went on for a while. Billy learned that Bob Tompkins worked at a meat packaging plant near Salina, Kansas. He worked on a line that butchered, apportioned, and shrink-wrapped cuts of beef for several nationally-known brands of meat. He was on his way to take his little girl to see the Rocky Mountains for the first time.

Things got really quiet for a while as they both stared into the fire, listening to the crackling logs.

Finally, Billy had to ask the question that hung heavily over them. "Mr. Tompkins…"

"Bob," said Mr. Tompkins.

"Bob. I don't mean to pry or to mess into something that's none of my business, but…"

"What happened to my daughter?"

Billy looked down, embarrassed.

"It's okay, Billy. I can call you Billy?"

Billy nodded.

"Car accident, three years ago."

"Oh, ok. Sorry."

"We were t-boned by a drunk driver in a big pickup. My wife was in the back, Angelica was up front. I don't remember why, now. He hit us really hard on the passenger side…ran a light. He was drunk and speeding. When I woke-up, the car was already on fire. I was able to get my daughter out…Susie…no.

"I tried…" Bob held-up his hands and Billy could see his hands were scarred up to his elbows, much like the left side of his daughter's face.

"Susie was your wife?"

"Yeah."

"Jesus, Bob. I'm sorry, I mean, I didn't want to make it hard on you. I'm sorry I asked." Billy felt terrible.

"No, no, it's ok. Really."

"So tell me about your daughter," said Billy.

"She is my life, man. I'd be nuthin' without her. She is the smartest kid in the world, top of her class; all A's in everything. Wants to be a doctor when she grows up. Math's her thing; she is way ahead of everybody in math. I mean; she knows stuff I can't even pronounce! You know, Pathagaram, or some such…I don't know. I am so proud of her! She is her mother; I'd swear they were twins. Look the same, talk the same… When I look at her, I see Susie. She's everything!"

Bob was beaming, shaking his head, waving his arms. "Right now, she's hung up on Disney; wants ta go ta Disney World. Well, meat packing isn't high pay, ya know. Now when her mother was here, we were doin' fine, we coulda done it. But now, I don't know. I'm savin' up, ya know. We'll make it someday… We live in Kansas; long way ta Florida. But I'll get her there; I'll get her there, somehow. Now I'm takin her to the mountains; she loves mountains. So that's something."

Billy was nodding his head all through Bob's excited speech. He asked, "Ok, I get the scars on her face, but why the wheel chair?"

"The crash severed her spine. She's paralyzed from the waist down."

"Oh, yeah…" Billy sat there thoughtfully a minute. "Did they get him; the drunk?"

Bob lost all semblance of his enthusiasm. "Yeah, he was injured, couldn't leave the accident, so they got him. He's doin' ten years in prison for manslaughter."

"I'd a killed the son of a bitch," Billy offered.

"I wanted to. During the trial, I just sat and stared hate at him, day after day." Bob was staring now, into the dying fire.

"Billy looked at him, "But, I don't see hate, or anger, or anything like that with you?"

"Billy, it's a fight. Every day it's a battle. It's hard, man."

"Do you forgive him?"

"Honestly, I'm workin' on it, but it's really hard."

"Well, then…why are you so upbeat? I mean, all evening, you're happy. I don't get it." Billy was confused.

"It wasn't like that for a long time," said Bob.

"What happened?" Billy asked.

"My best friend beat the shit outta me!" Bob started laughing.

Billy just looked at him.

"I was drinkin', I was mad, I was sick. I'd go ta work half tanked; it was bad," Bob began. "Well, one day, I showed up ta work drunk. I'm standing on the line, doin' my thing, doin' a shitty job, ya know. Guy next ta me could see it wasn't right. So, he calls Phil, the foreman, over an shows him what I'm doin'. Phil shuts down the line, sends everybody on break. Then he grabs my arm an' leads me to the restroom. He shuts the door an' he rounds on me; hits me square on the jaw, knocks me up against the wall between two urinals. I slide down the wall. I'm layin' there in piss and stink. He comes over an' he slaps me again.

Then he says, *'What the hell is wrong with you, Tompkins? You're screwin' my line! Makin me look bad!'* He slaps me again. Then he grabs me by the shirt an' picks me up, turns me an' slams me into the mirror; glass everywhere, ya know. He says, *'Tompkins, you have got to get it together! It's over man! She's gone. You can't bring her back! But you're still here and you have got to learn to live, man. If not for you, then for that beautiful little girl that you're blessed with.'*

Then he slaps me again. He says, *'God damn it man, you gotta live for her if nothin 'else! You are all she's got, you selfish piece of shit!'* He grabs me by the jaw and gets up close and says to me, *'I'm tellin' you right now! If you don't get it together and give that little girl everything she deserves, I'm goin' to court and I will take her from you!'* He slaps me again. I'm bleeding from everywhere.

Then he starts ta leave, and then he comes back and gets real close, and he says, *'Life is not fair Tompkins, I'm sorry Susie died. I'm sorry you couldn't get her out. I'm sorry! But that's over! Your little girl lost Susie too, you know.'* We're both cryin our eyes out now, an I'm bleedin', ya know. An Phil says ta me, *'Damn it, Bob!'* He says, *'You got choices; you can do good or you can do bad, you can be happy or you can be pissed. Bob, you can live in that damn, dark, filthy hole you're in now, or you can live in the Sun! Your choice! But if you choose wrong, I'm tellin' ya! I swear, I'm takin' your little girl away from you!"*

Bob sat quiet for a while, looking into the fire, and then looked at Billy. "Billy, I choose to live in the Sun. Phil's still the best friend I ever had."

Billy didn't sleep much that night; he kept going over the things Bob had told him. He couldn't help but think that he had had a pretty good life, all in all; short, but good. He felt a little ashamed of himself for his self-pity these last few weeks. "Everybody has trouble of some kind," he thought. He thought of Angelica, asleep in the tent in the next campsite. She was twelve; she was beautiful, on one side. She had to live with that a long time. He nearly started to cry. Then it came to him! "Isn't it somethin' how your mind'll fret; worry around things for hours; playin' with 'em, jugglin' 'em, rearrangin' 'em, testin' one thing or'tother. Then, BAM! Solution!" Billy went to sleep.

He was already boiling his coffee when Bob came out of his tent the next morning, looked at the sky and stretched.

"Mornin', neighbor!" called Billy, "Coffee?"

"Oh, that'd be good! Thank you!" Bob came trotting over.

"Where's your little princess?" asked Billy.

"Takes her awhile to wake up, won't be too long. She loves coffee! You have enough?" Bob looked at Billy.

"We'll make sure there's enough," laughed Billy.

After a few minutes, they heard, "Daddy?" from the other tent.

Bob set his coffee down and quickly returned to his daughter.

Awhile later, they came out of the tent, Bob pushing Angelica in her wheel chair. "Billy, you keep that coffee hot. We need to attend to some things, we'll be back." He waved. They turned away, heading for the restroom.

Billy saw his chance. He quickly went to the cab of his truck, opened the glove box and took out a fat envelope. Opening it, he counted out four thousand, five hundred dollars. He would still have more than enough to get home. He found another envelope, put the money in it, and searched the glove box for a pen. Finding what he needed, he quickly scribbled on the envelope of money, "Take your little girl to Disney!" He looked around to be sure nobody was watching or that Bob and Angelica were not returning. He then went to Bob's old van, opened the passenger door, and put the envelope into the glove box. As he did so, the van's registration fell out. He quickly picked it up and started to put it back into the glove box. Seeing the address on the registration, he quickly tore off a sliver of the envelope flap and wrote down the address.

By the time Bob and Angelica returned, the deed was done. The three of them enjoyed the coffee sitting together in a circle; Billy in his green and white lawn chair, Angelica in her wheel chair and Bob on the tail gate of Billy's truck. When the coffee was gone and the sun was well above the horizon, Billy offered his apologies; he had a long way to go. They all shook hands and bid each other, "God speed."

Billy waved as he drove out of the camp site, a broad grin on his face. He felt good. He felt better than any time in his entire life. He was overjoyed, euphoric! He had never done anything like that before and it felt great! As the miles wore on, he kept thinking about it, and he'd smile. But after a while, doubts began to creep in. Had he overdone it?

Would Bob and Angelica be insulted? Would they be angry and feel as though he was looking down on them; feeling sorry for them? He hadn't thought of that.

Would his act of kindness and generosity be perceived as an insult to these wonderful people he had just met? Then he remembered the address he had lifted from Bob's van registration. He could write a letter; explain why he had done what he had done. He was dying and didn't have anyone else to give the money to. That is what he would do!

Then another thought began to form in his head; he had a house, and a new truck, too! Who would get those when he was gone? Again, he began to get excited. The more he thought of the possibilities, the happier he got. He had a lot to do. He would need to see an attorney; create a will. The house needed work, oh boy, did it ever! But, he could do it. He would get it painted, inside and out. He would buy a new lawn mower, get rid of that old metal shed and buy a nice storage barn. He'd put new gravel in the driveway and get the front porch fixed, and paint it…get those ugly shrubs pulled out, and buy flowers to plant around the house. He could donate his mother's medical equipment to a senior center, or to a nursing home, or maybe there was a family in town who needed it! There was much to do! Would he have the time? He hadn't had a coughing spell in a while; maybe he had some time. Better go see the doctor, soon! "Well, get home, then!" He pushed the pickup to seventy-five.

Maybe life wasn't such a bitch, and everybody dies, someday. For Billy, it wouldn't be today.

Afterward

The hike was an awful struggle for Billy; he didn't remember it being that bad before. But, he hadn't been in the final stages of lung cancer before. He was on the Minister Creek Trail in his beloved Allegheny National Forest. He had decided this is where it was to happen. Where he wanted to go was not far; only a couple miles, but mostly uphill. He had to stop and rest every few minutes, breathing heavily, and terrified he would break down in gasping waves of uncontrolled coughing. He hurt, bad. In preparation, he had taken an extra dose of pain killers, but he wasn't at all sure they were working. He trudged on. With him, he carried a fifth of whiskey; Crown Royal, and his father's Colt's Model 1911, .45 caliber, semi-automatic handgun. There was only one round in the magazine; he didn't want some kid to find a loaded gun.

He finally made it to the top. The trail led along the edge of a steep drop-off to the right and a fairly open forest of tall beech and oak on a broad, relatively flat area that was the top of the ridge line of hills that went on and on, in repetition, from central Pennsylvania west to the Ohio River, from Maine south to Georgia and Alabama. These were the oldest mountains in North America and once rivaled the Rockies and the Alps in their grandeur.

As Billy walked along the trail, he looked for the opening in the underbrush that would lead to his destination. Finding the path, he turned right and stepped out upon a massive flat rock outcropping that hung over the edge of the ridge line and the deep valley below. He smiled as he looked at the vista before him. The valley stretched below to the left and right as far as he could see. Across the valley rose a matching ridge to the one on which he stood. He knew that on the other side of that ridge was another, and then another. It was a view unrivaled for many, many miles in any direction. He spent some time looking across the valley and remembering the times he had stood here with his father.

Finally, he turned to find a comfortable place on the rocks to sit. He was in no hurry; he would enjoy the Crown Royal for a while. Finding the spot he was looking for he sat and wriggled around to the most comfortable position possible. He took out the bottle of whiskey and twisted off the cap. He looked at the bottle, then tipped it up to his lips.

As he did, a movement in the weeds, across the broad rock, caught his attention. He watched quietly. Soon, the long fat body of a snake slid into view. The snake's body was greenish-grey in color, with a pattern of ragged black stipes wrapping around it; it was a Timber Rattlesnake; and a big one. The snake was coming out onto the great, open rock to warm itself in the Sun; even snakes prefer to live in the Sun. In the many times Billy and his father had been in these hills, they had never seen a Timber Rattler. They knew they were there, but never saw one. Billy was mesmerized.

The snake came out ten or twelve feet onto the rock until it reached a point where it was exposed to the full light of the sun. The Timber Rattler probably had a den under, or near the massive rock and made a habit of sunning itself each day on its surface. This was a large snake for its specie; nearly four feet long and as big around as Billy's forearm.

"Hello snake!" Billy said. Immediately, the snake began to coil and shake its rattle. It didn't hear Billy, but sensed the vibrations from his voice and reacted to the possible danger. Billy was not concerned as the snake was nearly twenty feet away. "You are the biggest rattlesnake I've ever seen," said Billy, then he tipped the whiskey bottle to his lips again. "Shit, you're the only rattle snake I've ever seen! And you are a beauty." He took another drink. With every vibration, the snake became more agitated, roiling its coils, rearing its head, and rattling its tail.

Billy sat studying the snake between drinks of whiskey for some time. As the minutes passed and the snake sensed no further vibrations, it lowered its head and quit shaking its rattle. An hour went by and the Sun began to lower behind the trees of the ridge on which Billy and the snake shared the rock. Billy had no real plan of action; he knew what he had to do. There was no turning back. Turning back only meant a few more days of no sleep, hard breathing, severe coughing, and intense pain. He did not ordinarily drink hard liquor; it was too expensive for him. This was a special case, and as the sun continued its descent, the whiskey did its work. Billy sat quietly. After some time he began to chuckle, and then he laughed drunkenly, and shouted, "I have a choice…the bullet or the snake!"

As the sun finally disappeared behind the trees, the advancing shadows slowly crossed the now unoccupied rock. The snake left first. Revitalized by the rays of the Sun, it answered its need to hunt and headed into the forest. Billy left soon after. He realized the rock was known by others and was not a place of privacy. He had only wished to spend a little more time recalling the life he had known. He wanted to witness one more time the beauty of this valley from this rock where his father had taken him as a child, to see the changing colors of the trees on the ridge across the valley as the rays of the setting Sun altered the Earth's atmosphere.

William Henry Morgan the Third was the last; there would not be a William Henry Morgan the Fourth. William Henry Morgan the Third had led a good life; he had enjoyed the love of a father and a mother. He had loved and honored them both in return. He had been given the rare opportunity to know the forest, the mountains, and the streams, and had been blessed to wander among them. He had cared for an ailing and helpless mother without hesitation, devoting his life to her when she needed him. He had learned the important value of purpose and of occupation to the human psyche and to the human spirit. He had seen the American West, or at least part of it. William Henry Morgan the Third had given everything he owned to a little girl from Kansas so she could go to Disney World and begin a series of operations that would restore her full beauty. Though much of his life was spent in the dark; at the end, William Henry Morgan the Third chose to live in the Sun.

Darkness fell on the forested hills of the Allegheny National Forest and the birds settled to rest for the night among the surrounding branches. The light faded and finally ended its color play on the trees of the distant ridge. The faint sound of the rills and falls of the stream in the valley far below echoed softly between the hills and the forest settled into another of a billion nights. And Billy didn't hurt anymore.

6

"Teacher"

fiction

"Artists are as fireworks; streaking ascendant into a darkened sky to burst forth in creative brilliance."

Asheville, North Carolina
October 2018

    Elliott came out of Malaprop's Bookstore in Asheville and looked up and down the street for her ride. It would not be hard to spot; it was a big, black limo. There it was, half a block up, occupying two parking spaces, the driver standing by the rear passenger door. Elliott turned back toward the store entrance, waved one last time to the store manager, then headed toward the limo. She was very happy… exhausted, but happy! It had been a great weekend…hectic, but great! The store had sold many copies of her new novel, *Wind Over Sunset Beach*. They did not have a final sales count when she left but would know in just a little while. However, Elliott was very tired and wanted to get back to the hotel – they could e-mail her the numbers later.

    The chauffeur quickly opened the door when he saw her coming up the sidewalk.

    "Good afternoon, Ms. McAllister. Did you have a successful day?"

    "I certainly did. It was awesome. Thank you, Phillip."

    Phillip smiled and nodded, then closed the car door as she settled into the luxurious passenger seat. Phillip slid into the driver's seat, turned to her and said, "You must be tired. There are drinks for you in the mini-bar. We should be back at the Inn in about twenty minutes, barring traffic issues. If you need anything, please ask."

    "Thank you," she replied.

    They pulled out into traffic and began their drive to Asheville's Omni Grove Park Inn, where she had spent the last two nights.

"This is decadent," she thought, watching the busy sidewalks of Asheville slide by.

There was no way she would have stayed at the Omni Grove Park Inn if Charles had not insisted. She thought back on the conversation she had had with her husband when she was first asked to do the book signing in Asheville. They had vacationed in Asheville some years before and had visited the Grove Park on the city tour. Now, she was doing a book signing and Charles suggested she stay there.

"Are you kidding? We can't possibly afford that. I'm sure Malaprops won't cover, like, five hundred dollars per night," she objected.

"We'll pay for it. You have earned it, you deserve it. Come on, it'll be fun," Charles insisted. "Look, *Wind Over Sunset Beach* has been on the *Time's* best seller list for five weeks! Your other two novels are beginning to take off, your anthology of *Great American Women* is doing well, and the twins are in their senior year of college, so those expenses will end soon. We can handle it. You're a star. Enjoy!"

"I wish you would come with me...," she pleaded, studying him sheepishly.

"I'd love to, but at the end of October, with quarter finals coming-up – I just can't this time. Besides, you're going to be overwhelmed signing books. I'd be bored to death," he replied, grinning.

Of course he was right; he would have been bored to death. It was hard to believe a college professor would have gotten bored spending two days in a book store, but Dr. Charles William Elliot was not only her much-loved husband, but he was also a very active outdoorsman, a well-recognized and published historian in his own right, and a greatly valued professor of American military history at the University of New Hampshire. In Asheville, North Carolina, he could have spent the three days of her book signing out hiking in the Smokey Mountains, but he would not have done that without her. She smiled thinking about all that. She smiled even broader thinking back to when they had first met and began dating at UNH. It was 1988, the beginning of her sophomore year and she had been invited to a frat party.

She noticed Charles right away. He was tall and skinny with unruly hair and wire-framed glasses, very studious looking. She was a bit of a scholar herself, also tall, with long, unruly auburn hair and freckles. She was not attracted to the jock crowd at all. She wanted to be a writer and she was very, very serious about that. Charles William Elliot was exactly the kind of guy she could fall for, but there was his name. Charles William Elliot!

They used to laugh and joke about it. If they were married, she would be Elliott Elliot! Even using her middle name, she would be Elliott Ann Elliot; it sounded like a law firm: "the legal partnership of Elliott Ann Elliot." Even using her nickname "Elli Elliot" was odd; it sounded like you were stuttering. In the end, when things truly got serious and they did get married, she kept her maiden name, Elliott Ann McAllister.

Phillip pulled up to the rather unassuming front entrance of the Omni Grove Park Inn and stopped. He quickly got out and opened Elliott's door.

"Thank you so much, Phillip. You have been so attentive and kind these last three days. I want you to know how much I appreciate it," she said, standing close by the door so he could not close it right away. He had to hesitate and look at her.

"You are most welcome, Ms. McAllister, the honor is mine," he replied graciously. "I will be here tomorrow morning at six to take you to the airport. It's about a half-hour drive, but you should be there in plenty of time to get through security and make your flight."

"Thank you!"

"You have a nice evening and get a good night's sleep, Ms. McAllister." Elliott stepped aside as Phillip closed the car door and climbed back into the driver's seat.

Elliott walked through the front doors into the grand lobby of the Grove Park. She decided she would have a drink before going to her room. She leisurely walked across the lobby to the bar and ordered a gin and tonic, then went to one of the rocking chairs placed in front of the nearest of the two grand fireplaces.

The main building of the Grove Park Inn was built entirely of native stone in 1912. The cavernous but beautifully designed two-story lobby, done in the Arts and Crafts style, was dominated on both ends by two jaw-dropping, massive fireplaces. A Volkswagen Beetle could be parked inside each one of them. Wood fires were kept burning from late fall through early spring. Logs for the fires could be eighteen inches in diameter and four feet long. There were rows of rocking chairs in front of each fireplace for the comfort and enjoyment of guests and visitors.

Elliott plopped down into one of these chairs to enjoy her drink. She leaned back and closed her eyes, reflecting on the last three days. She had arrived in Asheville Friday morning.

At one that afternoon, she had delivered a presentation to the assembled creative writing and journalism majors and faculty of the University of North Carolina, Asheville, followed by an extensive question and answer session. She then stopped by Malaprop's Bookstore and Café to meet the proprietor and to ensure everything was ready for Saturday's book signing, then to the hotel, dinner, and bed. Saturday and Sunday were a blur. She had happily greeted innumerable people, shook hundreds of hands, and signed uncounted copies of her book. Now, in reflection, she could not remember even one face of the many she had met. Sad, really, she thought. She felt a little guilty, but she never dreamed there would be so many.

She sat there with her eyes closed, absorbing the heat from the fireplace and feeling her muscles begin to relax. She thought about dinner, but wasn't really hungry. Maybe she would have a salad later. She really needed to call Charles. After sitting quietly for some time, she suddenly opened her eyes and stared into the fire, not really seeing it. In her mind, she was at a different place and in a different time. She needed to go to her room; there was something that needed to be done, something very important to her.

Pushing herself out of the rocking chair and picking-up her purse and jacket, she returned the empty drink glass and headed for the elevator located in the much newer, seven-story wing of the Grove Park in which her room was located. She pushed the elevator button for her floor and unexpectedly, the elevator immediately began to descend. The Omni Grove Park Inn was built on the side of a hill with the older, main building on the crest, and the two new wings built to the downside of the hill, at ninety degrees to each end of the original building, creating a massive "u" shape overlooking numerous terraced patios, the pool, the world-class spa, an outdoor restaurant, and the city of Asheville in the distance. Unlike most hotels, the room floors were below the lobby level of the original structure.

Elliott entered her room, put her purse on the dresser, and tossed her jacket on the bed. She looked at her watch; it was after five-thirty. Charles would certainly be home by now and anxious to hear how her day went. She decided to call him and then focus on the item that was presently uppermost in her mind. She went to her purse, retrieved her phone, plopped down onto the side of the bed, and pressed "Charles" on speed-dial.

After talking with her husband for over half an hour, she hung up, smiling. He was such a great catch, she mused. Again looking at her watch, it was now well after six. Still not hungry, she decided to get out of her uncomfortable clothes and into her pajamas. If she was hungry later, room service was available. After changing and wrapping herself in the luxurious robe provided by the hotel, she sat down on the edge of the bed again; it was time…

Elliott looked to the dresser for a moment, then got-up and grabbed her purse, bringing it back to the bed where she purposely upended it, dumping the contents onto the bed. She looked into the now empty purse, then reached down and pulled a well-worn and tattered envelope from the bottom where it had been securely fixed by the edges of the envelope snugly tucked against both sides of the purse.

Tossing the purse aside and again sitting in her former place on the edge of the bed, she stared at the yellowed and frayed envelope for some time, old memories beginning to rise in her mind.

On the front was written one word in elegant cursive, "Elliott." Within the aged envelope was a matching piece of stationery. Unfolding it, she read the few lines of cursive. Tears immediately came to her eyes and she unconsciously brought her free hand up in front of her mouth and began to quietly sob.

Lake Winnipesaukee, New Hampshire
June 1987

Elliott jogged easily along the quiet country road that led the three miles from her home to Mountain Lake Lodge. It was still early, 5:30 in the morning. The air had an early morning chill common to spring and summer mornings in New England. The slowly dissipating mist lay low along the shoreline of huge, freshwater Lake Winnipesaukee. She loved this time of the morning; it was quiet with little traffic, the tourists still tucked snuggly in their beds in all the cabins, lodges, motels, and bed-and-breakfasts that surrounded the lake. The road was hers alone but for the occasional critter or deer that she startled as she jogged along.

Elliott was tall and athletic with long auburn hair in completely unruly curls. She was thin and lanky with a strikingly beautiful face, blue eyes, and innumerable freckles, which she would be just as happy without. The three-mile jog barely raised her heart rate and she considered herself among the happiest people in the world. She was excited with her existence and acutely aware of the surrounding nature. She loved rural New Hampshire, the lakes and the mountains, and considered it all as her personal Adventureland.

Today was her first day of work for the summer. Her senior year had ended last Friday and she had selfishly relaxed over the weekend. Graduation was scheduled for the next weekend, but now it was time to get the summer under way; time to make some money so she could begin her first year of college in the fall.

Elliott McAllister had a plan. Her future was to be a writer; that was her goal and her dream, and there was absolutely no question in her mind about it. After graduation she would attend the University of New Hampshire, working summers and holidays at Mountain Lake Lodge to help pay for it, and then achieve a degree in creative writing and journalism. She would land a job with one of the major news outlets, or as a feature writer with one of the top periodicals, hopefully *National Geographic*, and travel the world. In her free time she would be a novelist and win a Pulitzer, maybe two.

Engrossed in her thoughts, Elliott turned off the road and jogged down the lane to the Lodge. She had worked all her summers at Mountain Lake Lodge since her freshman year, doing odd jobs and running errands, then as the cleaning lady and cook's help. This summer, she would continue cleaning the guest rooms each day and help the cook and owner, her Aunt Susan, with breakfast each morning, which was why she was at Mountain Lake Lodge before 6am.

Mountain Lake Lodge was a three generation Ross Family enterprise. It had been built in the 1890s as a hunting and fishing lodge for a club of wealthy businessmen from Boston.

Elliott's Great-Grandfather Ross purchased the property in the late 1930s. The lodge had been abandoned by the hunting and fishing club after the stock market crash in October 1929, and was in bad condition. Great-Grandfather Ross was able to get it cheaply through a sheriff's sale. He reconditioned the lodge, added more bathrooms, and reopened it to hunters and fishermen in the summer and fall, and to skiers in the winter. Susan and Elizabeth Ross's father grew up at the lodge and helped take care of it as a teenager. When he was twenty-one, he became a partner with his father. Over the years, the economic focus of the lodge turned to vacationers who came to New Hampshire to enjoy the state's natural beauty. They also enjoyed their amenities. Again, the lodge was updated.

The original eight rooms on the second floor were reduced to six in order to allow for the construction of a bathroom in each guest room. Eighty acres of the original property were sold to help pay for the upgrades, leaving twenty acres of forested land immediately around the lodge itself. Like their father before them, Susan and her sister Elizabeth grew up at the lodge until they each went to college. Their grandfather died in 1960, leaving the lodge entirely to their father. Tragically, in 1970, Mr. and Mrs. Ross were killed in an auto accident when a drunk driver hit them head-on.

It was decided that Susan would take over the lodge, as the oldest of the two sisters, at twenty-seven. Elizabeth, twenty-five, had just had a baby, Elliott, and had also just lost her husband in the Vietnam War. Susan successfully operated the lodge for the last seventeen years. She loved Mountain Lake Lodge and ran it well.

Arriving at the back of the lodge, Elliott rushed up the three steps, across the back porch, and through the screen door into the kitchen.

"Good morning, Elliott," came the greeting from the tall, well-proportioned, middle-aged lady, also with auburn hair, blue eyes, freckles, and a broad smile.

"Hi, Aunt Susan," Elliott replied.

"Boy, am I glad to see you," Susan Ross said. "Things are starting to heat up around here and I need help. I've got three rooms rented and breakfast for five this morning, but all six rooms rented for the weekend, eleven for breakfast both Saturday and Sunday. You can help, right?"

"I'm counting on it. I need the money," replied Elliott. "What can I do first?"

"There, on the counter, is a breakfast tray for number six. Take it on up to the room, please."

"Huh? Take it to the room?" Elliot was confused.

Mountain Lake Lodge was a bed and breakfast: people rented rooms for the night and had breakfast in the great room of the lodge anytime from 8:00 to 9:30 in the morning. Check-out was at eleven. There was no room service. In the three years Elliott worked for her aunt, she had never delivered breakfast to guests in their room, and certainly not before six in the morning!

"Yes, yes…I know, it's different…special circumstances. I'll explain later. Go ahead and take it up," Aunt Susan said dismissively.

Elliott went over and looked at the tray: special circumstances indeed, she thought, as she studied the tray's contents.

Two hard-boiled eggs, two pieces of buttered rye toast, coffee, and a large tomato juice with a lemon slice.

Normal fare at the Mountain Lake Lodge was a fruit cup, egg casserole with a tomato slice on the side, biscuits with butter, or toast, home-made hash brown potatoes, your choice of orange, grapefruit, or tomato juice, and coffee.

Elliott shrugged, figuring she would get answers later, picked up the tray, and headed through the swinging door into the great room of the lodge and up the open staircase to the second floor. She turned right onto the long hallway at the top of the stairs and walked to the end room, number six, or the "Martha Washington" room, as the guests knew it.

It was the largest and nicest room in the lodge and had a private covered balcony overlooking the Lake and the Belknap Range of mountains in the distance. Elliott knocked on the door and waited for a reply. After a while, she knocked again; and again, no reply. After knocking a third time, she carefully balanced the tray on her left arm and slowly opened the door, which was not locked, and looked in around the door. She was terrified she might surprise the guest coming out of the bathroom having just finished their shower. Across the room, she could see that one of the French doors to the balcony was standing open and through the curtains hanging over the full-length windows of the French doors, she could see the silhouette of someone standing on the balcony.

"Hello?" she called. The figure did not move. Again she called, "Hello?"

"Yes, what is it?" an annoyed voice finally replied.

"Sorry to bother you. I have your breakfast."

"Well, bring it here."

Elliott pushed the door fully open, crossed the room, and went out onto the balcony.

Across from the French doors stood a man looking out over the lake, his back to Elliott. He was tall and thin, wearing blue jeans and a light-weight gray sweater with the sleeves pushed up to his elbows. He had dark brown disheveled hair with a touch of gray at the temples. Elliott guessed him to be in his early fifties and, as he turned to face her, she was struck by his powerfully handsome face; long with a strong jaw, dark eyes that matched the color of his sweater, and heavy, bushy eyebrows.

The classic handsome face was tempered by a deeply furrowed brow, as though he was chronically troubled by something, and he seemed to be unusually pale. He did not smile or acknowledge Elliott beyond glancing at her.

She found herself staring and quickly broke her embarrassment with an awkward smile, managing a stumbling, "G-g-good, ah, good morning!" He did not return the smile, but pointed to the small side table by one of the deck chairs furnishing the private deck.

Elliott did not immediately register his meaning. He finally said, "There, put it there."

She nervously responded, placing the breakfast tray on the table, then straightened up facing him. She smiled again, but he had already turned back to the lake. She waited. After a pause, he glanced at her, "Was there something else?"

"Umm, no, I…" she started.

"Then, thank you," he said dismissively, absently waving her away with his hand.

Elliott hesitated half a second, tempted to stick her tongue out at him in return for his rude behavior. Thinking better of it, she turned and left the deck, passed through the bedroom into the hallway and down the stairs.

She burst through the swinging door into the kitchen, still red-faced from her encounter with the man in room six. "Who the hell is that?" she demanded of her aunt.

Aunt Susan turned from the counter where she was preparing the morning's egg casserole. "Who's what?" she asked, turning back to her casserole.

"Who the hell is the guy in six, why is he here, why does he rate breakfast delivery at 6 a.m. and what gives him the right to be an ass?"

"Well, nothing gives him the right to be an ass, but his name is Jonathan Steele. He's an author, and he is here to work on a book."

"Ok, I still don't get it," said Elliott.

Aunt Susan picked up a dish towel, wiped her hands, walked over to the kitchen table and sat down. Elliott, taking the hint, sat down across from her. "He contacted me several months ago. He lives in Boston and inquired about a long-term stay. Said he was an author and was having trouble concentrating on the book he was writing and thought he might do better in the country; less distractions. For what he offered, I couldn't afford to say 'no.' He's been here a couple of weeks already and he plans to stay the summer. As part of the deal, there were some unusual requests, like breakfast at six in the morning. Generally, he wants to be left alone. Like I said, for what he was offering, I couldn't say 'no.' He has been nice to me," she inexplicably blushed for a second, "Kinda quiet and stand-offish, but not rude."

"Well, he was rude to me," Elliott put in.

"You sure you're not over-reacting? Maybe he was just concentrating on his story…didn't really mean to be rude.

Later, when you go up for his tray, maybe he'll be better. Give him a chance."

Elliott hoped her aunt was right as she ascended the stairs to retrieve the breakfast tray from room six. She had helped Aunt Susan prepare breakfast for the regular guests and had cleaned up the table and washed the dishes while Susan took care of check-out. Now, the only ones at the lodge were the three of them; Aunt Susan, Elliott, and the man in room six, Jonathan Steele.

Elliott had been thinking about Mr. Steele all morning; the name seemed a little familiar, but she couldn't place him. He was a writer and she wanted to be a writer, so there must have been a connection; surely she had heard of him somewhere.

After the guests had left she brought up the subject again to Aunt Susan who told her that Jonathan Steele was generally an historian and focused on non-fiction, although he had also written some "fiction-based-on-fact" historical works. Susan really got Elliott's attention when she said that Steele had won a Pulitzer some years ago for a work he had done on international leaders of World War II. Steele would be staying at the lodge all summer. Elliott truly hoped that she would get along with him; maybe he could give her some pointers on how to become a successful writer.

As she approached room six, she was both relieved and disappointed to see the breakfast tray sitting in the hall outside the door. Curious, she inclined her ear toward the door, but could not hear any activity from inside the room. Sighing, she picked up the tray and returned to the kitchen. The rest of the day was spent cleaning the guest rooms and laundering the sheets, towels, and pillow cases. When she asked about doing the laundry for Mr. Steele's room, Susan told her that she would take care of that; it was part of the deal between Susan and Mr. Steele.

She did see him again during the day, as it was his habit to go for a walk each day along the shoreline of the lake behind the lodge. He would spend time sitting in the gazebo Susan had built when she first took over the lodge after her and Elliott's mother's parents were killed. Elliott saw Jonathan in the gazebo when she glanced out the window of room four, the "Dolly Madison" room, while making the bed. Getting along with Jonathan Steele would have to wait until breakfast the next morning.

Promptly at 6 am the next morning, Elliott carried the tray set with two hard boiled eggs, two slices of buttered rye bread, a glass of tomato juice with a lemon slice, and a cup of coffee up the stairs, down the hall to room six, and tapped on the door.

As was the case the previous morning, there was no response. She knocked harder:

"Yes?" was the irritated response through the door.

"Your breakfast, Mr. Steele," Elliott called out.

"Yes, yes. Bring it in."

As she opened the door, Jonathan glanced up from the table where he sat in front of a word processor.

He was dressed much as he had been the day before, and turning back to the work at hand, he simply waved toward the bed and said, "There."

Elliot crossed to the bed, prepared to set the tray on it as requested, but then realized that to do so would result in spilled tomato juice and coffee. Instead, she chose to put the tray on the bed stand. As she turned to do so, she noticed two wine glasses already occupying the stand. "Odd," she thought, "why two glasses?" but picked them up with one hand and replaced them with the tray.

Turning to go, she noticed several sheets of typing paper on the floor around the table where Jonathan had dropped them. Holding the wine glasses by their stems in her left hand, she leaned over to pick up the papers with her right.

"NO!" shouted Jonathan. "Don't touch those!"

Elliott jumped back in shock, backing away from the table where Jonathan sat and bumping against the bathroom wall, nearly dropping the wine glasses.

"I'm sorry, I was…," she managed.

But he cut her off. "Leave those alone! I'll take care of them! Thank you," he said abruptly. "If there is nothing else, I'm working."

Elliott quickly left the room and ran down the hall, crimson-faced, tears streaming down her cheeks.

• • •

Jonathan sat in the over-stuffed chair in his "Martha Washington Room," his head lying back against the top of the chair, eyes closed. There was a tap on the door bringing Jonathan's head up. He looked at his Rolex, 9:30pm, just as he expected. He got up from the chair, crossed to the door and opened it.

"Hi. How are you feeling tonight?" asked Susan, standing at the door in a dressing gown, open at the front and nothing on underneath, two wine glasses in one hand and a bottle of dry Riesling in the other.

"Much better now, thank you," replied Jonathan with a rare grin.

Later, after the long, warm, slow intimacy climaxed with shuddering intensity, and the whispering small talk faded, Susan and Jonathan sat naked in the chairs on the private deck, the remainder of the Riesling and two fluttering candles sitting on the side table between them. The evening was warm for June in New Hampshire. It was quite dark and quiet, there being no guests this evening; there was no one in the lodge but the two of them.

Susan said, "You know, I'm very angry with you."

Jonathan looked over, surprised. "Angry at me? Why?"

"You have been really quite nasty to my niece."

"I'm sorry, I don't understand," replied Jonathan.

"The girl who brings your breakfast each morning is my niece, Elliott," Susan said, pointedly looking at him. "You treated her terribly."

"Your niece…? Come to think of it, I thought I saw a resemblance. Mean to her? How was I 'nasty' to her?"

"You were very short with her and you yelled at her the other morning. She came back downstairs crying," Susan said, raising her voice slightly.

"Well, I was working, and she interrupted me. You know how focused I am when I'm working. And then she was going to throw away some of my drafts. You know I can't have that. What if someone should find them in the trash? They could steal my work! I have to be very careful," insisted Jonathan.

"Still, you didn't have to yell at her. C'mon, she's young. How's she supposed to know about copyright laws and all that?" asked Susan.

"Well, someone should teach her…" replied Jonathan. "I'm sorry I yelled at her," he said softly, looking away.

Susan leaned forward in her chair, inclining toward Jonathan, and looked at him intently. "Yes, someone should teach her."

Jonathan looked back at her, bewildered. "What…?"

• • •

Jonathan swiveled his chair from the cheap side table his word processor was perched on and faced the tall, lovely girl standing away from him by the door. He could tell she was uncomfortable, even scared; her hands were behind her back and she looked down at the floor, her face flushed, as a guilty child standing before the principal awaiting punishment. He studied her for a moment, then asked, "Susan said you want to be a writer, is that right?"

"Yes," came the hushed reply. She did not look up.

Aunt Susan had sat Elliott down to talk the morning after her discussion with Jonathan concerning his outburst and rude behavior. Susan knew she needed to intervene in order to not lose Elliott's help for the summer. But more importantly, Susan realized that Jonathan and Elliott were very much alike and that he could really help Elliott as a writer, if indeed that was her passion. Elliott reacted to the idea of Jonathan becoming her mentor with a resounding "NO!" It took several days of cajoling, reasoning, and an agreement that Elliott could immediately bow out if things went south for her, before she agreed to give it a try.

So here she stood, completely vulnerable and totally uncomfortable, in the presence of this man she considered to be arrogant, rude, a bully, and her enemy. She fully expected a repeat performance of his last tirade and stood ready to bolt through the door, which she had purposely left open behind her to facilitate her escape.

Jonathan understood the situation perfectly; as an author and an artist, he had years of experience and an acute sense of situational perception. He knew that if he was to maintain his positive relationship with Susan, along with the perks and fulfilled needs that accompanied it, he had to make amends with this girl and offer her his artistic help. He realized, though she did not, that his future success and comfort, limited as it was, lay in the hands of this girl. He dropped his gaze to the floor in front of him, lowered the volume of his voice, and said, "I guess I owe you an apology for shouting at you the other day, I'm sorry about that."

Well, this was totally unexpected. She was prepared for a lecture, not an apology. She looked up at him in surprise. "Uh, it's ok…I guess," she replied.

After an uncomfortable pause during which neither knew quite what to say, Jonathan repeated his question. "Well, is it true? Do you want to be a writer?"

"Yes." Elliott responded, a second time.

"Ok," Jonathan came back. "First lesson: writers are very jealous and protective of their work; they cannot allow it to leak to the public before they are ready to publish. Discarded manuscripts meant to be thrown away, shredded and destroyed, may contain lines of value. So, that is why I was so abrupt with you the other day when you started to pick up the papers on the floor. I'm a known writer. Had you thrown those papers into the trash, it is possible someone might have fished them out. The composition I am working on might have been compromised. Your intention was generous, thank you. Also, you interrupted my train of thought. I over-reacted. Again, my apologies."

"No problem," said Elliott.

"Please, sit." Jonathan pointed to the well-used, commercial, stuffed chair in the corner. She did.

"Have you written much as yet?" he asked.

"Just what has been assigned in creative writing class at school and some poetry. I keep a journal," Elliott answered.

"Would it be ok if I was to read it, the school material and poetry? I understand the journal is private."

"Sure," Elliott replied, shrugging, trying to be nonchalant, while thinking, "Oh my god! My stuff is going to be read by a famous, Pulitzer Prize winning author! Oh my God!"

"I have one question to ask, then I'll let you go for today. Why do you want to write?"

With her previous thought uppermost in her mind, she answered, "I want to be a famous author, like you, and have movies made from my books, and go to book signings, and win awards, like the Pulitzer!"

He sat quietly a moment, looking at her. Finally, he smiled and absently picked up a pencil lying on the table. He studied the pencil for a while, then said, "Well, thank you for the compliment. It's all fine and good to want to be a success at anything you commit to, admirable even. But if your goal for any endeavor is the prize you may win from others, then you will fail."

"Shit," she thought, "bad answer, I'm an idiot." She felt like crying.

He looked up at her crestfallen face. Obviously, she was embarrassed. He smiled, "Don't feel bad. Your response was a normal one; most people would have said what you did. It's not a problem." She looked relieved.

"But, if you want to be a successful writer, you need to look deeper. There are no guarantees of reward at the end of your efforts; the reward must be the work itself. Therein is the satisfaction. Anything you receive beyond that…well…it's just stuff. Nice; but just stuff. If you write for the reward and the approval from others, you invite disappointment, frustration, and discouragement. You can never be happy or satisfied with your work. You will languish and you will fail." He could see she was confused, "You think about this for a while, okay? And bring some of your writings, okay?"

The interview was obviously over. Elliott stood up to go, turning toward the door.

Jonathan stood as well and stepped toward her. "Hey," he said, and extended his hand, smiling. "Thanks for coming. You have a great day."

She looked up at him, then shook his hand. "Yeah, thanks," she said, smiling back.

Elliott and Jonathan agreed to meet twice each week, Tuesdays and Thursdays. These would generally be among the slowest days of the week for business at the lodge, making it easier to free Elliott from her chores. Susan was very amenable to making the schedule work as she was the primary instigator of the whole arrangement. She also called her little sister Elizabeth, Elliott's mother, to make sure the arrangement had her approval.

Elizabeth McAllister could easily pass for Susan's twin, though she was two years younger. She, too, shared the auburn hair and freckles of the family, and was tall and strikingly attractive.

She was an elementary school teacher in the local public school system and spent her summers working for the local AAA as a part-time employee during the busy season. Elizabeth knew Jonathan through her sister and was aware of the relationship between the two, but did not know Jonathan was spending the summer at Mountain Lake Lodge. She did not like Jonathan much. She did not understand why Jonathan had never married Susan, yet seemed to always be central to her life. She thought he was using Susan and told her so on many occasions…history.

Jonathan's approach to mentoring Elliott was more as a philosopher than an instructor. He wasn't interested in tutoring her in grammar or spelling or any of the nuts and bolts of the art of writing and literature. He was more interested in guiding her in a more analytical direction. They would meet in the late mornings, Elliott taking an hour or so from cleaning rooms. Susan was happy to pick up the slack. Occasionally, on rainy days, they met in in Jonathan's room, but more often, they sat and talked in the gazebo by the lakeshore, or they walked along the lake or along the lane to the town road.

Jonathan would often talk of nature, or point out some tree or bird and ask Elliott of her thoughts or impressions at that moment. He might ask her about historical events or ask her why the lodge was built the way it was. And he would expound extensively on various topics, perhaps for the length of their meetings. These discussions confused Elliott; she could not understand what these topics had to do with becoming a writer.

At least once each week, Jonathan would bring up a subject or point out an object of interest. They would discuss it, and he would ask her to write about it; a paragraph or a page or two to bring to him the next week when they would review her work together. He would make suggestions for improvement, but he always approved her work and complimented her. Invariably, he would ask her at some point, "Elliott, why do you want to write?" Eventually, out of exasperation, as it seemed anything she might say was not the answer he wanted, she began to simply reply, "Because!" She wished he would stop asking.

He spoke of life experiences and their value in an author's work. He told her that an author could be found within his or her work, as they often put parts of their own personality into their stories and developed their fictional characters by giving them traits of their own personality, habits, and foibles. He explained that many authors provided authenticity by writing about what they had personally experienced. Jonathan taught Elliott that writing was an art, like music and painting; as a painter created a composition through the arrangement, repetition, variation, and contrast of shapes, shades, and colors, or as a musician created a musical composition by arranging, varying, and contrasting timed notes, rests, and key changes; so an author arranges, contrasts, and repeats words, paragraphs, and punctuation to create a composition of power and meaning. These, the elements and principles of composition, are universal within the arts. Jonathan also gave Elliott a reading list of several contemporary works as well as classics. He instructed her to read the local newspaper, choosing an article each week for them to digest and critique together.

In early July, during one of their walks along the lane leading to the Lodge, he asked what she thought about human creativity. Her honest reply, that of a high school student, was, "Not much, why?"

"Well, do you think it's important?"

"Important to what...who?," she replied, thinking, "Oh God, here we go again! What are you talking about?"

He chuckled, looking down to the gravel lane as they strolled along. "Well, we all have it, you know."

"I suppose..." she said, leading him on.

They walked several more steps before he said anything. "Elliott, creativity may well be the greatest gift man has ever been given. It may be the one thing that brings us closer to God, if you believe in God. It is by no mistake that the Bible says, "God created Heaven and Earth...," and that we call this unique ability, this gift; creativity."

"It is a seed within each of us, within every one of us; we are all born with it. A seed, like an acorn is the seed of an oak tree. That little acorn that you can pick up, hold within your hand, and can easily throw a distance, if it is watered and nurtured, can become an oak two hundred feet high and live for five hundred years. Our little seed of creativity, if watered and nurtured, can lead us to build the Empire State Building, or to paint the Mona Lisa, or write *War and Peace*, or..."

"Okay. I get it! I get it," she said, turning to him. They stopped walking and both laughed in relief at the intensity of Jonathan's soliloquy.

Then he looked at her quietly for a moment, turned, and started walking again. "Yes, Elliott, you get it, but as a writer, an artist, you need to know that creativity is the foundation for the design of every appliance that enhances our world, our lives. Creativity is the paint that colors our existence." He stopped walking again and faced her.

"Each of us is born with the seed, the gift of creativity, and, remember this: with that gift, we all dream, most wonder, many reason, but only those who act are remembered. Those who do not meet their own creativity, who do not water and nourish the seed… well, do not become…oaks. Elliott, I know you do not understand my meanderings these last several weeks, or our discussions, or why I asked you to write about why the lodge was built here. Elliott, I am feeding your seed, and so must you. You must look around you, at everything. You must notice everything and ask yourself, 'why?' 'Why is it there, what is its story?' Elliott, to be an artist, a writer, you must feed your seed!"

• • •

Other than her discussions with Jonathan, Elliott's summer was mundane; arrive at the lodge before 6 am, help Susan prepare, serve, and clean up the breakfast, and clean the rooms, along with the attendant laundering of towels, sheets, and pillow cases. She generally finished her day around four in the afternoon. She walked or jogged to work in the morning, but always walked home again, because of being tired and the warm June and July temperatures.

She always had dinner with her mother, spent time perusing the newspaper, reading one of her assigned books, or working on her own writing. She would spend an hour or so before bed sitting on the front porch with Elizabeth enjoying the evening air with a glass of wine. Weekends varied little from weekdays and she did not stray far from home. She had school friends with whom she would occasionally meet for ice cream, or go to a movie, but not often. Both Elizabeth and Elliott worked hard and money was tight. They wanted for nothing, but certainly could not be extravagant. Besides, both were saving for Elliott's college.

Each morning, as she passed through the gravel parking lot on her way to the kitchen, she noticed the forest green Jaguar sitting in an open space, away from overhanging trees, and wondered if it belonged to Jonathan. She meant to ask him, but had always forgotten by the time they met to talk. One morning while preparing breakfast, Susan confirmed it was his. "Humph, a Jag! Must be nice," Elliott thought.

"Do you think you and your mother would be able to handle the lodge next Monday?" asked Susan.

"I dunno, okay by me," said Elliott. "You need to check with Mom. It'll mean she'll need to come here after work and make the casserole for Tuesday morning. I can handle most everything else."

"Yeah, I'll call her," Susan confirmed.

"What's up?," Elliott asked.

"Hmm? Oh, uh, Jonathan asked if I could drive down to Boston with him. He has to see his agent."

"Okay." Elliott wondered why Susan would need to go with Jonathan to see his agent, but didn't say anything. The very next week, Susan again asked if Elliott and her mother could take over, and the week after. This soon became a regular routine. Always, it was to see Jonathan's agent. Elliott didn't care much, but she thought her mother would get upset and begin to object, but Elizabeth did not. Actually, Elliott really didn't mind. Nearly every other trip, Jonathan brought her a book from a Boston bookstore.

She did notice several times when Jonathan and Susan returned, Susan was driving and Jonathan didn't look well; very pale, washed-out, and distracted. When she asked if he was all right, he would smile and say he was a bit car sick, but would be fine after a nap and went to his room. Innocently, Elliott let it go.

• • •

"Elliott!" Jonathan exclaimed, suddenly turning toward her with a surprised expression on his face. "Elliott!"

They were sitting in the gazebo by the lake for their Thursday morning session.

"What?" she said, with an equally surprised expression on her face. She began to giggle at the situation and the goofy expression on Jonathan's face.

"Elliott!"

"Would you stop? You're being weird," she said through her giggles.

"We have been meeting all these weeks, and just now it hit me what an unusual name you have for a girl! Why is your name Elliott?"

"It's my dad's name."

"You're named after your father? Why?"

The giggles stopped and Elliott suddenly flushed and turned her gaze out across the lake.

Seeing her discomfort, Jonathan turned serious and apologized, saying, "Oh; sore subject; sorry."

"No, it's okay, just not something we talk about a lot," she replied.

"Oh – 'we' being you and your mother?"

Elliott nodded in affirmation, still focused on the other side of the lake.

"Why?" asked Jonathan.

Now Elliott shifted her gaze to her hands which were clenched on her lap. There was a long silence. "My dad is dead."

"Oh, Elliott, I am so sorry, I'm sorry I asked." And Jonathan picked up the book lying beside him that he had purchased for her on his weekly trip to Boston, for it was time to change the subject.

"He was killed in Vietnam," she continued.

"I see…"

"He was killed right before I was born, so Mom named me after him; in his honor."

"So you never knew him. Does your mother tell you about him, or talk about him?"

Now the tears began to slide down Elliot's cheeks; she shook her head.

"Well, surely, she has she told you who he was, or shown you a picture of him?" Jonathan asked quietly.

Elliott wiped away a tear rolling down one cheek, "She showed me his picture in his uniform once."

Jonathan looked at her intently; he was shocked. Why hadn't Susan ever told him about this? This poor girl was eighteen years old and had no idea who her father was, other than her father was killed in Vietnam. "She has never told you anything about him? How he died? Where he was from? How they met? What he was like? What about his parents, your grandparents? They are part of your life, right? Where are they? Where do they live? I mean, has your mother never told you anything about your father?" Jonathan's voice became louder and grew in intensity with each question, his disbelief and frustration with Elliott's mother uppermost in his mind.

Elliott began crying openly about halfway through his barrage of questions. As he finished his interrogation, she jumped to her feet, facing him, "Why are you asking me this? It's none of your damn business! Why? Just leave me alone. Why are you such an asshole?" she screamed. She turned and ran up through the yard, past the lodge, across the parking lot, and up the lane.

Jonathan stood up and watched her go. "Well, now you really have something to write about," he mused to himself.

• • •

"You really are an asshole! What were you thinking?" Susan's face was as red as her hair, her freckles standing-out dark against her angry and flushed face. "What the hell is wrong with you? You had no right to confront Elliott about a personal issue that you know nothing about."

From the kitchen porch, Susan had also watched Elliott run across the parking lot and up the lane, crying. She knew that Elliott had been with Jonathan in the gazebo. She went through the kitchen heading for the front deck and intercepted Jonathan coming up the front steps to the deck. He told her what had happened.

"I had no intention of pursuing the issue. I even tried to change the subject," Jonathan defended himself.

"I asked you to help her with her writing. I did not think you were going to interfere in her life. You had no right. It was none of your damn business!"

"What did you just say?" Jonathan had been assuming the stance of a beaten puppy to this point. He felt terrible about what had happened. He had grown fond of Elliott and certainly did not want to hurt her. But at the same time, he was shocked and angry at Elizabeth for not telling her daughter about who her father was. If he had overstepped, surely Elizabeth had no right to hold back half of who Elliott was in order to not have to face her own pain. So when Susan said that he had no right to interfere in Elliott's life, it struck a chord that went to the heart of who he was. The attitude of a beaten puppy was no more.

He looked down at Susan and stepped toward her. "You made it my damn business! You asked me to help her become a writer. You asked me to do this even as you knew I have cancer and it meant extra effort and strain. You asked me to do this when you knew I did not want to!" He took a deep breath and turned and stepped away from her.

Then he turned back. "What did you think; that I was going to teach her how to spell? Teach her how to hold a pen, or to type, or where to put commas and colons? Art is entirely about interfering in people's lives. It's about disturbing them. It's about making them ask questions, awakening their curiosity, their creativity; it's about making them think…awakening their spirit!"

He took a step closer to her now and made a motion with his two hands together as if he were digging. "It's about reaching into their heads and their hearts and stirring things up. And that can be painful." His voice now dropped in volume though not in intensity, "It's about advancing humanity!" His shoulders now dropped, as if he was spent with exhaustion.

He looked at Susan and continued quietly. "Elliott needs to discover who she is, to learn of, and know herself. How can she possibly do that by knowing only half of herself? How can she discover herself without knowing where she came from, without ever knowing her father? And, why? Why didn't you ever tell me about this?"

Susan stood and heard Jonathan out. The more she listened, the more she realized that he was right. The confrontation about Elliott's father was unintentional. Too, it was wrong of Elizabeth to hold back from Elliott the knowledge of her father all these years. It was certainly time for Elizabeth to face her own demons and to let her daughter know her father. It was a mistake that had gone on for far too long. And, she should have told Jonathan about Elliott's father. When Jonathan had finished, Susan looked at him and said, "You're right. I'm sorry, Jonathan."

Jonathan took a big breath, turned from her, and walked several feet down the deck. He took another big breath, turned and came back to her. "No, no! I'm too intense. I should not have fired all those questions at her, I'm sorry. I feel awful. She may never come back."

"It'll be ok, don't beat yourself up too much. I'll talk to her if needed," assured Susan.

Jonathan stood there with his hands in his pockets, head down, shaking his head.

"Hey, I have one more question." Susan stepped up to him and put her arms around him.

"What's that?" he asked, returning her embrace.

"What do you want for dinner tonight?" she asked.

He grinned. "You!" was the playful reply.

"Hah!" She gasped, feigning shock and playfully slapping him. "I'll have guests tonight; we have to be quiet."

"We? You're the one who makes all the noise!"

. . .

Jonathan worried that Elliott would not come back. He understood that, in time, she would understand her pain was not from him. He had merely scraped away the scab of an already deep and festering wound. Still, he felt very badly and wanted to talk with her. But she had to come back only when she felt ready. He also expected a visit from an irate Elizabeth. Already, she did not like him because she disapproved of his relationship with Susan. This wasn't going to help her like him any better. Two weeks went by, and he waited.

On the third Thursday after the incident in the gazebo, he came to his room after his morning walk along the lake and nearly stepped on a stapled manuscript that had been slipped under his door. He picked it up and looked at the front sheet. Typed across the center of the paper was "*Elliot McAllister, My Father.*"

Elliott's biography of her father was superbly written and touching; far beyond the competent recitation of assigned topics she had given to Jonathan to this point. Her heart was here and the work was, undoubtedly, emotionally difficult for her to write.

"*My father died August 4, 1969. I was born August 10, 1969. My name is Elliott McAllister. My mother named me for a father I always loved, but never knew.*"

Jonathan read the entire work in one sitting, without stopping to edit or to correct spelling or punctuation. It was engrossing, it was passionate, it was brilliant. It relayed the life of Elliott's father and the shared life of he and

Elizabeth. It presented Elliott's perceptions and her dreams of who her father must have been with the little she knew of him for so many years.

Elliott wrote of the many nights she would go to bed, sneaking the photo of her father into bed with her. She described the many hours spent looking at the photo and inventing stories about him, always making him the hero of her imagination, her knight in shining armor; the ideal father of her dreams. She wrote of a weekend of pain, turmoil, and love that passed between Elliott and her mother when Elliott came home and confronted Elizabeth after her incident with Jonathan in the gazebo.

Jonathan was drained when he finished reading Elliott's work, but at the same time, he felt much better. He was relieved that his confrontation with Elliott had led to something good; the resolution that had to someday happen between Elliott and her mother. He was proud to have played a positive role in that resolution and was glad that Elliott was in the process of forgiving him for stirring in her life. Perhaps the lessons would now continue. He hoped so, for the work he now held in his hands demonstrated that Elliott would be, and already was, a gifted and thoughtful writer.

She knocked on the door with "Martha Washington" written on it. From inside came the invitation, "Come in!" She opened the door and walked in. Without looking at Jonathan, who sat at his word processor, she crossed the room to the over-stuffed chair and sat.

He swiveled his chair and watched her cross the room.

Neither spoke for some time. Finally Jonathan said, "Elliott, your story is beautiful; it is brilliant."

She put her hands to her face and cried.

• • •

The summer moved on uneventfully, from July into August, for those at Mountain Lake Lodge. It had been an unusually dry summer, the agreeable weather bringing many more visitors from the large population centers to the south. The income this produced was welcomed by Susan, although it meant more work for her and for Elliott. Susan did not allow the uptick in visitors to interfere with Elliott's Tuesday and Thursday, late morning lessons with Jonathan.

For his part, Jonathan now had a far greater confidence and respect for Elliott's talents, resulting in a more rigorous and cerebral approach to their discussions. He interspersed philosophical theories, humanitarian quandaries, and sociological "isms" into their discussions, as well as critiques of artistic works bearing deep themes of realism. At first, Elliott was overwhelmed by the discussions and often found herself at a loss to the point Jonathan was trying to convey, only to find, to her frustration, that he had no point beyond challenging her. More and more often, as the lessons passed, she asked increasingly searching questions, and by August began to anticipate the next lesson with follow-up questions.

She would lie awake the night after a particularly deep discussion, pondering the world that was opening to her. Her follow-up questions began to take on the form of "Well, if given this, then why not that?" Jonathan's lesson preparations began to ease as Elliott began to actually prompt the discussions. She found she really enjoyed her time with Jonathan and felt he was the smartest person she had ever known. She was amazed how much he knew about so many different things. How could he remember it all? She was in awe of him and looked forward to their time together.

Another of the summer's routines carried on without great explanation, that being Jonathan's and Susan's weekly trips to Boston. Elliott continued to accept Jonathan's excuse of motion sickness without question; however, she did begin to notice that deep into a particularly sunny summer, he seemed to retain his pale complexion though he continued his daily morning walks. Toward the end of July, she had begun to notice he might not completely finish his breakfast, something that never happened earlier. She was not aware of his eating habits for lunch or dinner as Susan handled those meals.

Had she known, she would have been alarmed. Jonathan was now on a controlled diet, dictated by his doctors, and often could not complete the meals Susan prepared for him. He wrote less and napped nearly every afternoon. The weekly trips were, of course, for his chemo treatments.

During Susan's night-time visits, which also became less frequent with Jonathan's deteriorating health, she and Jonathan talked about the possibility of letting Elliott in on their shared secret regarding his declining health. Susan believed it was terribly unfair to not tell her, as Elliott and Jonathan were becoming close, but Jonathan insisted that Elliott not know, at least for a while.

When Jonathan was first diagnosed, he determined not to let the cancer defeat him or to allow it to interfere in his career. He was a heavily published author and lecturer, and was particularly known socially in New York and Boston. When the doctors finally got his attention, their prognosis concerning his case and its outcome were dire. There would be a continuous deterioration.

He had to make some decisions. He did not want sympathy or the publicity his circumstances would produce. He certainly did not want to continue his active social life just to have his colleagues and associates consoling him each time they saw him, or to have the tabloids follow his inevitable demise with their shocking photos tracking his gradual physical deterioration. So, what to do? He decided to announce that he had started on a particularly demanding work that would require extensive travel and enforced solitude. Then he called Susan at Mountain Lake Lodge and arranged a weekend with her in April.

The lodge was not new to him; he had visited there often, particularly in the winter, when there were few guests. Susan and he had been lovers for over twenty years. They met when Susan was a college student and he held an associate professorship at the University of New Hampshire. Of course, Susan was devastated by his medical prognosis, which he did not tell her until he arrived the weekend to make the necessary arrangements to complete his plan. Through her tears, she agreed to help him in whatever he needed and promised she would stay by his side as long as he needed her, no matter what. She also agreed to back his plan and his excuse for the extended stay at the lodge. Neither of them had anticipated Elliott.

As they so often do, unexpected circumstances forced conclusions.

"Susan, I'm not going back." Jonathan sat in the passenger seat of the Jaguar, pale and shrunken. He felt awful, had not said anything as they drove out of the parking garage, out of downtown Boston, around Manchester, and up Interstate 93.

Susan turned her head from the road and looked at him. She knew exactly what he meant, but did not want to accept the inevitability of what his words would mean. She looked back at the road, then out the driver side window, and wiped her eyes with her left hand.

"I'm sorry," she finally said, "you're not going back?"

"You know what I mean," was the quiet reply as he turned his head to watch the southern New Hampshire landscape pass by. Nothing more was said the rest of the way to the lodge where Jonathan went straight to his room.

• • •

They were sitting on the large covered deck outside Jonathan's room. He had been describing to Elliott how the interrelationship of science, engineering, and art was not an anomaly in the mind of Leonardo Da Vinci alone, but rather, an often unrecognized truism of humanity. They had a coffee table book on the works of Leonardo and were studying excerpts from Leonardo's Leicester Codex describing his studies and experiments on water currents.

The day, like those preceding it for several weeks, was dry and unusually warm, which explained why they were not sitting in the gazebo. Besides, it was easier to see the book's pages out of the sunlight. The deck overlooked the lake; a little over a football field's length from the shoreline. To the southwest, the atmospheric low that would bring the welcomed break to the drought was gathering strength as it advanced to the northeast, guided by the prevailing jet stream that had crossed North America, west to east, for millennia. Had either Jonathan or Elliott looked out to the lake, they would have noticed the darkening sky in the distance. They continued their study, for a time.

It was the light but accelerating breeze that first caused Jonathan to look up as the trees began to answer the demands of the coming storm. As a tuft of hair brushed across her face, Elliott, too, heard the rustling of the leaves and felt the heavy humidity begin to lighten. They both looked out across the lake at the advancing darkness. Elliott closed the book and made a move to get up to go into the lodge, out of the weather. Jonathan caught her wrist.

"Wait a bit, let's watch it come," he said.

"But shouldn't we go in where it's safe?" Elliott asked.

"It'll be fine. We are protected here. Let's watch the storm," assured Jonathan. Elliott sat back down.

Each watched the approaching disturbance quietly, absorbed by Nature's developing drama.

The distinct line of quickly moving, ink-black clouds, contrasting sharply with the azure blue sky it gradually obscured, advanced low across the distance toward the lake and the lodge. The leaves of the trees moved lightly at first as the cool air from the front began to arrive, then more violently as the air from the cold front quickly slid under the stagnant humid air it encountered before it. Jonathan and Elliott watched as the rain shield reached the far side of the lake, first sharply outlined against the darkening distance, then becoming misty and indistinct as the rain's curtain began to close over it. Then it was gone, invisible behind the moving wall of the downpour. Eerie to watch, the downpour crossed the lake, raining hard just a few hundred yards away, but still dry at the lodge.

A blinding flash of light caused the voyeurs to jump, immediately followed by a booming crash of thunder, as a powerful bolt of lightning exploded a large, tall, centuries-old, white pine barely half a mile to the north of the lodge. The splinters of pine flew in all directions as the tree was truncated to half its past glory.

The wind and rain engulfed the lodge, thrashing the roof and the windows, in seeming rage at the interruption of its descent to the parched ground below. The wind now tossed the limbs of the trees surrounding the lodge in a wild and crazy dance, furiously shaking the summer leaves and desperately trying to tear away the fragile verdant foliage.

Most of the leaves, stronger than the wind, grasped tightly to their slender stems, while others, losing their tenuous hold, blew away in the tempest. A few lighted upon the rain-wet porch before the observant two, and stuck damply to the deck flooring not far from where Elliott and Jonathan sat in awe. Rain pounded the overhanging roof of the deck and cascaded from the edge in torrents within seconds of the loosing of the gale.

The two sat deep in against the wall of the lodge, twelve feet from the edge of the overhanging roof, yet the wind-driven mist still reached them. It was light, not enough to force them into the shelter of the lodge; rather, it provided a cooling, welcome chill after the weeks of hot drought. It is doubtful either would have moved anyway, as they sat transfixed by the power of Mother Nature's performance. Moving fast, the raging tempest did not last. The concentrated force of the cold front soon swept by them, to relieve the hot, dry weather of regions further to the north and east. With its passing, the wind moderated, the deluge lessened, and Jonathan and Elliott could again see out from their shelter to the lake and vaguely across to the other shore.

A steady, light rain continued after the storm, promising a prolonged period of needed moisture. It prattled comfortably against the over-hanging roof. They sat quietly, their tension relaxing as the violence ended. Elliott was about to say something to break the quiet between them and release her nervousness from enduring the storm.

"Wonderful!" shouted Jonathan, startling Elliott almost as much as had the storm. She quickly looked in his direction. He was sitting on the edge of his chair, his eyes gleaming, a broad grin on his face.

"Wonderful! Incredible! Amazing!" He looked at her and began to laugh. Then his voice dropped in volume but increased in intensity as he shifted his gaze from her to across the lake. Elliott knew the visage and realized she was in for a philosophical soliloquy.

"To be so honored! My God! What beauty! What power!" A pause. "To be so honored!" Jonathan's gaze was focused on something far away.

"A symphony to the senses. The slight welcomed fragrance of the coveted rain born upon the freshening breeze. The fun, frantic jump of the unsuspecting leaves, exposing their lighter undersides, then blushing dark green again, as if embarrassed. Flitting about in the breeze, just to be violently jumbled in every-which-way as the wind tried to destroy them! The deepened blue-black of the approaching front; massive, intimidating, overpowering, threatening in speed as it came upon us. The grey curtain of rain, oddly dousing the lake yet nary a drop at the lodge, then suddenly, each drop pounding all around us in their trillions. The whole storm, like Tchaikovsky's '1812 Overture,' starting softly, building with intensity then crashing with the sound of great guns in battle!"

Jonathan's voice had resumed its great volume, like the storm, like Tchaikovsky's overture, like great guns in battle. Unconsciously he spread his arms wide. "And the lightning and thunder! As if Mother Nature was crying forth, 'I am here, you foolish, fragile beings! Abide my wonder! Abide my power! I demand your attention! Abide and respect my beauty, my softness, the utter infinity of my being from the smallest electron to the vastness of the unending universe! You belong to me and you are nothing without me! Enjoy the gifts I grant, fear the disasters of my wrath!'"

Jonathan was spent, his arms fell down to rest on the arms of the chair; he finished in a whisper, "My God! To be so honored! What beauty! What power!" His clenched fist moved in emphasis to his words.

Elliott was looking at him in amazement, almost frightened, wondering if Jonathan had gone into some kind of trance. She had witnessed him expound on a topic before, but nothing like this!

Jonathan sat quietly for a while, then looked over to Elliott, then smiled sheepishly, "And you, young lady, are a beam of sunlight on this rainy day. You look lovely, sitting there." He chuckled, got up from his chair, and then added, "So, go home and write about the storm, Elliott."

Elliott continued to stare. She said nothing. She was mesmerized.

. . .

Walking home from the lodge, Elliott was in turmoil. It was a crush, she knew that in a practical sense, and she chided herself to not be a foolish school girl with a crush on her teacher. "Come on. He is over thirty years older than me." But then again, wasn't a crush a kind of love? Well, just a few minute ago, didn't he say she was 'a beam of sunlight' and that she 'looked lovely?' Or, was he just being nice? "Ah, stop it," she said in exasperation to the trees that lined the road on one side and the lake to the other. She looked up at the sky and covered her face with both hands, then shook her head in disgust, telling herself, "Get over it." In just a few weeks, she was headed to freshman orientation at UNH. She probably would never see him again. Again, she told herself, "So, get over it!" And, as soon as she thought it, she knew she couldn't. She laughed, "Wishful thinking!" She began to count the few Tuesdays and Thursdays left before she departed for college, the little time she would spend with him.

Those lessons; that precious time, flew by. There were five more lessons, and though Elliott tried to concentrate on what Jonathan gave her, she had a hard time. And as much as she watched Jonathan during those lessons and focused on his face, memorizing it in the innocent, adolescent fear that, with time, she might forget, she missed that he grew more pale each day. She missed that his face became a little more gaunt each day, his beard and hair a little more grey at the temples each day, and that he became a little thinner each day.

She brought his breakfast to his room each morning and each morning he greeted her with a big smile and, "Good morning, Elliott. You're a beam of sunlight on a rainy day." She cherished that greeting each and every day, and the few moments of small talk between them that followed, even on days it did not rain. She missed that not all the toast was eaten, or shrugged off as no big deal that the hard boiled eggs were not touched. She ignored that only a few sips were taken from the tomato juice, or that the cold cup of coffee was still full. She did notice the weekly trips to Boston had ended.

• • •

    Susan decided there needed to be a celebration; a party to mark the beginning of the next phase in Elliott's life; a send-off to her further education. A celebration to honor a successful summer, for the coffers of the lodge, and for the success for her pet project: Elliott's summer education under the tutelage of her long-time lover. A celebration; a desperate attempt to raise Jonathan's spirits, for though he presented an air of enthusiasm, especially around Elliott, Susan knew it was an act. Although Elliott missed Jonathan's deterioration each day, Susan did not.
    Susan noticed the unfinished breakfasts, and the missed lunches. She shared the evening dinners with him when he could not eat at all and, in the middle of a conversation, fell asleep in the chair on the deck outside his room. There were no more evenings of love-making followed by sitting naked on the deck with a bottle of wine. Susan was terrified of what she knew was to come. When Jonathan came to stay at the lodge, she had been happy. For the first time in their long relationship, she actually had Jonathan with her and she made the most of it.
    Over the late spring and summer, she was able to, almost, put his condition out of her mind. He was hers,

finally; for a time. Now, as fall came on and Jonathan's condition began to manifest; reality set in. Jonathan was hers, but *IT* was taking him from her and there was nothing she could do.

• • •

It would be a wonderful dinner, a wonderful celebration. Susan planned the hot dishes: New England clam chowder, lobster tails with melted butter, fresh asparagus seasoned with garlic and pepper and covered in a cheddar cream sauce, and cheddar-mashed potatoes. Elizabeth agreed to bring home-made biscuits, a tossed salad, and angel food cake with raspberry sherbet for dessert. Jonathan called his favorite vintner in Boston and ordered a bottle of the finest sherry, two bottles of dry Riesling, and two bottles of Dom Perignon, delivered to the lodge. No price was too much to see his prize student off to her life's adventures!

The evening of the celebration arrived. There would be the four of them for dinner, Susan, Jonathan, Elliott, and her mother, Elizabeth. Jonathan had not seen Elizabeth in several years, knew she did not like him and was very anxious at the greeting she might have for him when she arrived. Of course, Susan had anticipated this and had prepped her sister as to Jonathan's condition and begged her to be on her best behavior.

• • •

For her part, Elizabeth's attitude toward Jonathan had mollified over the summer. Initially, she was not at all certain she liked the idea of her one and only child being under the philosophical influence of Jonathan, who had been stringing along her sister for twenty years. At Susan's assurance that she would act as chaperone, Elizabeth agreed to give it a chance. Now, she was glad she had; Elliott had obviously grown and matured. In recent weeks, as the two of them sat on the front porch with their wine before going to bed, Elliott would spend an hour or more enthusiastically telling her mother about the things she had learned from Jonathan

The clincher for Elizabeth came the Thursday evening when she got home from work to find a very upset, tearful, and angry daughter who confronted her demanding to be told everything about her father. After hearing about the incident in the gazebo, Elizabeth nearly stormed out of the house and drove to the lodge to confront her daughter's tormentor. However, the pleading expression on her daughter's face made her hesitate. And when Elliott, tears streaming down her cheeks, took her hand and pleaded, "Mom, please," her heart melted.

It was a three Kleenex box night for the two of them followed by a weekend of crying, sobbing, laughing, and hugging. Elizabeth went to the attic and brought down a box that contained all the memorabilia and memories she had tried to put behind her. She brought out her wedding dress, which Elliott had to try on. It fit. Together, Elliott and her mother went through photo albums of Elizabeth and Elliot's wedding and honeymoon, yearbooks, and packages of yellowing photos, and Elizabeth finally told her daughter who her father was.

At the bottom of the box was a small rectangular container covered in dark blue velvet. Elizabeth picked it up and handed it to her daughter. "This is yours now," she said softly, reverently. Inside the little box was her father's Purple Heart. By the end of the weekend, Elizabeth realized that Jonathan was not a tormentor, but a teacher for Elliott, and, perhaps, a liberator for herself.

• • •

Elizabeth opened the kitchen door of the lodge and she and Elliott brought in their packages of biscuits, vegetables, dressing, cake and sherbet. Laying it out on the kitchen table, Elizabeth turned to Susan who was stirring the clam chowder. "Hey Sis!" Where's Jonathan?"

Susan looked at her apprehensively, "Now Liz…"

Elizabeth smiled. "It's fine, really! I want to thank him."

"He's in the great room making a fire."

"Elliott, stay here and help your Aunt. I need to have a parent-teacher conference with Mr. Steele." Elizabeth turned and went into the great room.

As the door opened and Elizabeth came into the room, Jonathan got to his feet in front of the stone fireplace. Looking at the stern expression on Elizabeth's face, he thought, "Oh shit, here it comes! Jeez Liz, don't screw-up this up for Elliott!"

Elizabeth crossed the room and stood looking up at Jonathan, then extended her open hand and said, "Thank you, Jonathan. Thank you…for both of us."

It was a wonderful evening. They moved one of the dining room tables in front of the fireplace, Susan and Jonathan sitting on one side, Elizabeth and Elliott on the other, so that all of them could see the fire. The food was fantastic. It was an expensive treat for them all, starting with the clam chowder, then the tossed salad, followed by the main course: lobster, cheddar potatoes, and asparagus. Conversation was upbeat and lively, Elliott doing most of the talking; telling stories of the summer and explaining the courses she would be required to take her first semester.

The other three tried to give her tips on how to get along at the University of New Hampshire, which then led to reminiscing about their college years. The Riesling was soon gone and it was time for dessert. They all agreed they were too full and decided to wait an hour or so. The women cleaned up dinner and Jonathan built up the fire. Then they sat in the two over-stuffed, leather love seats that now replaced the dining table in front of the fireplace. Jonathan finally said, "I think it is time for toasts!" He got up, went to the kitchen, and retrieved a bottle of Dom Perignon from the fridge. Opening it, he gave each of them a generous pour and stood by the fireplace.

"A toast! To the smartest, loveliest student I've ever had. May your future be bright, your troubles few, and your friends true!" They drank and Jonathan sat down beside Susan.

Elizabeth poked Elliott in the ribs with her elbow, "Jonathan. After spending a summer trying to teach my goofy daughter how to be a writer, tell me, really, is she any good?"

"Mom!" Elliott smacked her mother's knee, embarrassed.

"Who? Her? She's terrible," Jonathan said laughing.

"Jonathan!" Elliott screamed, throwing an over-stuffed pillow at him. Elizabeth poked her again and they both started laughing.

Jonathan waited until they stopped giggling, and said, with a serious look on his face, "Elizabeth, she is as good as I ever was…"

Elliott immediately turned to her mother laughing and shouted, "Ha! See, I told you so…" and in so doing, missed what Jonathan said next, "…and better than I ever will be…"

Elliott missed it; Susan did not. She reached over and covered Jonathan's hand with her own.

• • •

"Amo, amas, amat, amamus, amatis, amant! Ahhh! Oh, my God! Whatever possessed me to take Latin?" exclaimed Elliott, sitting at her desk in her dorm room.

"I tried to tell you, but nooo; you didn't listen," said Amanda, Elliott's roommate, sitting at her desk on the other side of the room with her back to Elliott.

"Yeah, yeah…you were right. But, I need this to expand my vocabulary," replied Elliott. "It's just, I have a quiz tomorrow and I have to conjugate fifty verbs. Fifty! Not ten, not twenty, but fifty. How's that a quiz, not a test? If we just didn't have to cover so much, so fast."

"Hmmm…" said Amanda absently, who was already back to her trigonometry.

Elliott had hit it off right away with her new roommate from Cambridge, Massachusetts. Amanda and Elliott were roomed together because they were on the University of New Hampshire women's cross country team. Not only were they roommates and teammates, they did pretty much everything together. Everything but classes; Elliott was on a liberal arts track in preparation for a journalism major;

Amanda was planning to become a chemical engineer. Amanda was a very smart girl. She also was an only child, the daughter of an engineering professor at MIT and a mother, like Elliott's, who was a school teacher. Where Elliott was tall with auburn hair and freckles, Amanda was of medium height, of Mediterranean origin, with a fine, olive-skinned complexion, huge eyes, jet black hair, and drop-dead gorgeous.

Summer had quickly turned to fall, as is common in New England. Elliott became immersed in all there is to be as a college freshman and she was having a good time; her only issue was her struggle with Latin.

The weeks were flying by, each day occupied with an early, controlled, and healthy breakfast followed by a six-mile run with her teammates. Then back to the dorm for a shower, then classes. Elliott's classes were over by 1:00 in the afternoon, after which she had lunch. Her afternoons were spent in her room or at the library. At 4:00, cross country practice began and ended at 6:00. After dinner, she studied or socialized in the dorm.

Most Friday nights were occupied with attending films, concerts, or dances sponsored by the school or a fraternity. The girls were up again early on Saturdays for a breakfast that centered on steak and eggs in preparation for their cross country meets. Home meets were usually over before the weekly football games which the girls always attended together. Saturday nights were again spent at concerts, dances, or other social events. Sundays were for study and preparation for the coming week.

Both Elliott and Amanda were very attractive which occasionally created complications. Sometimes these complications were welcome, sometimes they were not. But being nearly inseparable worked in their favor, for it was difficult for guys to approach one of the girls without the other coming to her partner's defense. Both girls were too academically focused to let themselves become romantically distracted during their freshman year; that could, and would, come later. They very soon worked out a series of signals to let each other know whether the impending approach of a man was welcome or not. It worked very well for them both.

・・・

"Elliott, you have a guest." The intercom on their dorm phone interrupted her conjugations. She expressed her frustration, "Ahhh!"

Thinking it might be a guy, Amanda offered to go down and put him off.

"No, let me see…" said Elliott, picking up the receiver connecting her to the dorm's reception desk.

"Hi, who is it?," she asked.

"A second…" the volunteer replied; Elliott could hear the girl's muffled voice asking the guest who they were.

"It's your mother," the receptionist came back. Elliott was shocked. "My mother?" she said rhetorically. "Tell her I'm on my way down."

She put the receiver down and looked at Amanda, who had immediately turned from her work, worried at what this might mean for her friend.

Quickly getting up from her desk, Elliott threw over her shoulder, "I'll let you know," as she left the room and started for the steps.

"Mom! What are you doing here? What's wrong?" Elliott urgently asked, crossing the lobby to the reception desk.

Elizabeth's face was lined with concern. She looked at Elliott with worried eyes. "Is there somewhere we can sit alone?" she asked.

Now frightened, Elliot said, "Well yeah, over here…" and guided her mother to a bay window alcove with a window seat and two over-stuffed chairs positioned to look at the landscape beyond the dorm. "Mom, what's wrong? Is there something wrong with you? Are you sick? Is Aunt Susan okay?"

Elizabeth held up her hands and shook her head, then said, "Elliott, I'm fine, Susan is fine. Please sit down." Then she sat in one of the chairs. Elliott looked around for a second and then sat on the window seat facing her mother. Elizabeth sat for a few seconds looking at her daughter, not saying anything.

Elliott impatiently said, "Mom!"

"It's Jonathan, Elliott."

"Jonathan? What's wrong with Jonathan?" asked Elliott.

"Elliott, Jonathan passed away last night," said Elizabeth.

There was silence. Then Elliott half laughed, "What, Jonathan? What?" She started to shake her head.

"Elliott…" Elizabeth started, but now tears were flowing down Elliott's face.

Elliott started to get up. She was crying and shaking her head, "But…no, no, this is not funny, Mom…stop it, just stop it!" She was now standing with her hands over her face. Elizabeth stood and put her arms around her.

• • •

A thorough man, Jonathan had made arrangements soon after the doctors informed him of his diagnosis. His body would be cremated and interred in a vault in a cemetery in Laconia, New Hampshire, to be near Susan. There would be a brief interment ceremony. A memorial service in Boston would be required as he was a nationally recognized author and had a large group of friends in Boston society.

Susan came out of her private apartment from changing her clothes after the private interment ceremony. It had been a week since Jonathan had died and, thankfully, the brief services at the cemetery were not as difficult as she had expected. Only the five of them had attended; Elizabeth, Elliott, herself, the undertaker, and the pastor of Elizabeth's Lutheran Church, who graciously agreed to do the service, as Jonathan did not belong to a church.

She crossed the great room of the lodge and went through the kitchen doors. Elliott was sitting at the kitchen table waiting for her. Susan stopped and the two of them looked at one another for a few seconds. Finally, Susan smiled and said, "I guess it's time for us to have a talk. I guess I owe you an explanation." Elliott didn't say anything. This was not going to be easy; Susan looked at her watch. It was 2:30 in the afternoon. "Well shit, it's five o'clock somewhere."

She crossed to the refrigerator, took out an already opened bottle of Riesling, and took two glasses down from the cupboard next to the fridge. Returning to the table, she filled both glasses, sat one in front of Elliott and sat down in the chair across from her.

"Why didn't you call me?" demanded Elliott.

Susan took a drink, "I wanted to. He wouldn't let me."

"I don't understand, why wouldn't he let you?" Elliott ignored the glass of wine in front of her and never took her eyes off her aunt.

"I asked him if I could call you several times over the last month when he really started getting bad. He got angry with me. He said 'No! I don't want her to see me like this.' The day before he died, I begged him to let me call you; he kept shaking his head 'No.'"

"You should have called me, Aunt Susan!"

"Elliott, I'm sorry."

"What the hell happened? I don't understand any of it!" Elliott was deeply hurt and exasperated.

Susan took a long sigh followed by a good gulp of wine. "Elliott, Jonathan and I knew each other for a very long time, over twenty years."

"You told me he was just an author looking to write a book and needed solitude. You never told me you knew him for a long time. You lied to me? Why did you lie to me?" Elliott was angry.

"I know, I know. That was the way he wanted it. Elliott, I am so sorry. That was what he wanted. He didn't want anyone to know he was here; he didn't want anyone to know he was sick. I agreed not to tell anyone. We didn't know the two of you would become friends. Later, he didn't want you to know how bad he was getting." Susan was now pleading with Elliott. She desperately wanted Elliott to understand. She hesitated, then said, more quietly, "Elliott, he didn't want anyone to know he was sick because he didn't want anyone's pity. Elli, it was cancer; it was really bad. There was nothing they could do." Susan paused, looked down into her wine glass, then turned sideways in her chair and wiped her eyes with her hand. Sighing deeply, she turned back to the table, and looking into Elliott's unwavering eyes, she haltingly said, "Sweetheart, Jonathan came here to die."

Elliott jumped up, knocking her chair over backwards behind her. She started pacing back and forth across the kitchen, then stopped back again at the table and looked down at her aunt, her hands on her hips, thinking, considering. Finally, she picked-up her wine glass and took a big drink of the Riesling, reached down and righted the chair, sat down and firmly placed her hands palm-down on the table. "Ok, tell me! I want to know all of it, please!"

"Well, ok. Where should I start?"

"How did you two know each other?"

Susan sat quietly for a moment, sipped some wine and then began. "We met at your school, UNH. I was a freshman; he was an assistant professor of history. I knew when he walked in the first day of class that he was 'the one.' I made sure to ask a lot of questions, especially after class. I made sure to study hard and get good grades in his class. I basically set him up; I went after him." She chuckled. "We started seeing each other and fell in love. It was wonderful, of course! I never met anyone like him…there is, was nobody like him. We'd spend weekends in a cabin in the Green Mountains; go hiking, eat out, make love. It was awesome. We went to Woodstock in '69; bet your mother never told you that, huh? We were probably the oldest ones there."

Susan was smiling now, reliving a good time in her past. "Jonathan was kinda into Janis Joplin and Arlo Guthrie. He heard they were going to be at this outdoor concert in upstate New York and asked if I wanted to go. Well, hell yeah I wanted to go!

We had no idea what we were getting into, nobody did. We had to park, like, four miles from the site and walk in…didn't see the car again for three days. I have never seen so many people. They had to bring in food, and helicopter out people who got sick. To sleep, we just laid down under some trees." She paused, remembering, laughed again, and blushed. "We went skinny-dipping in the pond there; it was the only way to take a bath and wash our clothes. Ha, right in front of everybody!"

"Well, if you were in love all those years, why didn't you ever get married?" asked Elliott.

"We did!" Susan blushed and held up her left hand so Elliott could see the ring on her fourth finger. "We got married a couple weeks after you went to college. I guess he wanted to make an honest woman out of me," she joked.

Elliott's mouth had dropped open. "He waited all these years? He waited until he was ready to die, then asked you to marry him?" She took a big drink of wine.

"Don't be too harsh on him, Elliott. You have to understand; he was already married."

"What?" Elliott's eyes nearly popped out of her head.

"No, no, not what you're thinking; not to another woman. He was married to what he was."

"Huh?" Elliott was confused.

"Jonathan was a true intellectual. Come on, you've seen how he was when he really was captured by a subject, really into what he was doing. Well, that's what he was married to. I couldn't compete with that. I didn't realize what a problem it was until after I graduated. We decided to try to live together; got an apartment and played house. He damn near drove me nuts. He'd be up all night writing something then sleep all the next day."

"He couldn't keep a schedule. I'd wake up some mornings and he would be gone. There would be a note on the kitchen table, 'need to do some research, I'll call.' But he'd forget to call, like, for a week. And when he did, he called from Texas, or some godforsaken motel in South Dakota. It just didn't work."

"And then my parents were killed in the car wreck, leaving this place up in the air. Somebody had to handle it. Liz had just had you and lost your dad, so it fell to me. Truthfully, I didn't mind. I love the old place. And, you know, things happen; time went by, we kept seeing each other when we could. He got an apartment in Boston. I ran this place…life happens."

"Then, the beginning of September, he asked. I said 'Yes.'" She stopped, looking at the ring on her finger, "Sooo, here we are."

"You've loved him all this time? After a while, didn't you think you should find someone else?"

Susan looked up into Elliott's eyes, "I told you, I never met anyone like him. He was 'the one.' And I don't regret a minute of it."

"Wow!" said Elliott quietly, staring at Susan

"There's something else, Elliott. I need to tell you about you. It's really important that you hear this and that you understand it," said Susan.

"What?" asked Elliott?

Not sure how to start, Susan poured herself some more wine, and thought for a moment, playing with the ring that was still new to her finger. "Look," she said,

"Jonathan and I were lovers; we loved each other for twenty years. I've never loved anyone as much as I loved him; and I know he loved me. But Elliott, now listen and understand." Susan stopped looking at her ring finger and looked into Elliott's eyes.

"Jonathan loved you very much. But, it was different, not like he loved me. Maybe he loved you for the daughter he never had, I don't know. But, I know he truly, deeply loved you. When he came here to stay, I would go to his room in the evenings. We'd have dinner and sit on the deck outside his room and talk. After you started taking lessons with him, he started telling about what the two of you talked about. As the summer went on, that's all he talked about. And when he did, the pain went away, the hurt went away; the sickness went away. His eyes would shine and he would get so excited... The thing is, he was happy then. He was happy with you. You gave him that, Elliott. For those short few months, you gave him back his happiness. You gave him a reason to live again." Susan reached across the table and took Elliott's hand, "Thank you."

Susan was smiling, tears running down her cheeks. Elliott felt like her chest would explode!

Suddenly, Susan broke the spell, "Oh shit!" she said, "I almost forgot. Jonathan gave me a letter to give you." She got up from the table, went into the great room to the guest desk, took out the letter and brought it back to the kitchen. She handed it to Elliott.

Elliott looked at the letter with her name carefully and beautifully written on the center of the envelope. She looked up at her aunt, then back at the letter. Then she jumped up and ran out the kitchen door.

She ran around the lodge and headed down to the gazebo where she had spent so many hours with Jonathan. It was the end of October in New Hampshire; the cold was penetrating and the wind was biting. Crisp, brown leaves of late fall blew by Elliott as she ran toward the gazebo. She did not see the leaves. She did not feel the chill of the wind nor the sting of the cold. Sitting down on the gazebo's bench, she looked through the condensed cloud of her own breath at her name, so carefully and beautifully written on the letter. Then she opened the letter.

Asheville, North Carolina
October 2018

Elliott awoke with a start as the alarm on her phone went off. She quickly leaned over and grabbed the phone, fumbling to turn off the alarm. She managed to silence it. Setting the phone back down on the bed stand, she stretched out her arms and then rubbed her eyes. Lying there, staring at the ceiling, it took her a few seconds to comprehend her surroundings. Remembering where she was and why she was there, she quickly grabbed her phone again and checked the time. No problem, she had given herself plenty of time to shower and get ready before catching her ride to the airport. She checked her texts and was relieved to see a notification from the airline; her flight was on time.

She sat up on the edge of the bed and looked around for a few moments. She had fallen asleep the night before without even turning down the covers. She had slept through the night on the bedspread. Lying in the middle of the bed, surrounded by the contents of her purse, was the tattered envelope and treasured note. She stared at the note for a moment, then picked it up and read it:

Dear Elliott,

    I am sorry I could not have stayed longer to help you more.
    It was not to be.

    Artists are as fireworks,
    Streaking ascendant into a darkened sky,
    To burst forth in creative brilliance;
    Granting light and beauty
    To where was shadow and sorrow.
    Then to fade, leaving the warmth of afterglow
    In the hearts of those whose souls
    Their light has touched.

    Your creative brilliance will be brighter,
    The warmth of your afterglow enduring
    Far longer in the hearts of those who love you.
    You are of a deeper humanity.

    Feed the seed of your creativity and you will be a great writer.

    Ellie, why do you want to write?

        Love,
        Jonathan

Elliott sat quietly for a few moments, then, to Jonathan only, she whispered, "Because, I must."

She folded the note, placed it in the envelope and secured it at the bottom of her purse. She then replaced everything that had been emptied out the night before and went into the bathroom to get ready to go home.

There was a knock at the door followed by, "Ms. McAllister, it's guest services. I'm here for your luggage!"

Elliott quickly opened the door. "Your timing is perfect; I'm ready. Thank you."

She looked around the room one more time, went through the door and headed for the elevator with the attendant following behind.

She crossed the lobby to the front desk and checked out. Phillip was standing by the main lobby doors holding an umbrella. Apparently, it was raining.

"Good morning, Ms. McAllister. You sure are a beam of sunlight on a rainy day. You look lovely today," exclaimed Phillip as Elliott approached the doors.

Elliott stopped dead in her tracks several feet from Phillip and stared at him. The smile suddenly dropped from Phillip's face. Had he said something wrong? Did he offend this important guest?

Elliott quickly recovered from the unexpected but well remembered greeting. It had been a shock to hear it. Seeing Phillip's consternation, she quickly stepped up to him and, smiling broadly, placed her hand on his arm and looked into his eyes. "Phillip, thank you so very much for that, it means more to me than you can know."

Relieved, Phillip relaxed, smiled and regained his professional composure. He then turned and opened the door for her. He held the umbrella expertly over Elliott's head, protecting her from the morning's light, misty rain as they approached the limo. Assisting her into the rear passenger seat of the car, Philip then shook and closed the umbrella and quickly slid into the driver's seat. They left the Omni Grove Park Inn and drove slowly up the curved entry drive on their way to the airport.

7

"Sanctuary"
Fiction

Sanctuary: a place of refuge; a place of safety; a place of peace.

He liked to watch the dust fly up in front of him as he walked along. He had cut off the tops of the toes of his old Converse sneakers months before; they were too small for him and pinched his toes. As a result, the loose front ends of the sneakers flopped a bit, catching the pale, tan New Mexico dust and throwing it into the air as he walked along. The other result was filthy feet, ankles and legs; but he didn't mind, he would wash them off later. Besides, the flopping and flying dust kept him entertained as the miles went by. It didn't take much to keep him entertained; he noticed the simple things, like the flying dust, that most people would ignore or, at most, would find annoying, irritating, and bothersome. But Anthony just smiled at it, played with it, even openly laughed at it.

Anthony noticed the simple things because he was "simple." Anthony was also big; six feet, four inches tall, and at least two-hundred and forty pounds. He had thick legs, kind of stubby, and heavy, massive arms and shoulders. The strong muscular arms and shoulders were those of someone used to years of heavy labor, day in and day out. He had an upper body that matched his arms and shoulders, yet an athletic waist and hips. He was of Italian descent with dark skin made even darker by the unrelenting Sun of the American Southwest.

His face was long and full; heavy lips over a rounded jaw, a wide long nose, and deep-set eyes that seemed to permanently squint with dark heavy eyebrows. His forehead was short and heavily wrinkled, both from the constant squinting and the effects of his hard, stressful life. His family was from southern Italy, so his hair was dark and curly, and in great need of the attention of a barber. Though Anthony was only twenty-four, he looked much older and his facial expression made him appear as though he carried the accumulated worries of all mankind on his shoulders.

He trudged forward, focused on the path ahead of him; his eyes squinted, brows knit, forehead wrinkled, mouth drooped open, and sweat running down his features. He wore a pair of old faded blue coveralls with both legs cut off raggedly above the knees, an old once-white t-shirt full of holes, and the toe-less Converse, with no socks. He wore no hat, despite the bright Sun, because he did not own one. He carried an empty khaki, Boy Scout knapsack.

The only break from his focused intensity was when he noticed the flying dust. Then, his manner changed to that of a child; grinning, laughing, kicking the dust. But it lasted only for a moment, then the drudgery overtook him again. The trail was long; eight miles from the ranch near the bottom of the escarpment to the town ahead. Eight miles in the ninety-degree heat on the dusty trail though the dry creosote bush of the southern New Mexico wasteland.

It was ten in the morning. He had started nearly three hours ago, early, to beat the worst of the heat, and now he could see his destination through the rising, rolling waves of heat ahead: Sanctuary, New Mexico.

• • •

Upon appearance, Sanctuary, New Mexico, seemed to be a very unlikely place for sanctuary. Story was, it was named over one hundred years ago by an old prospector who got lost and was searching for water in the arid climate. Apparently, he stumbled upon a rare spring among an outcropping of rocks, surrounded by pinion pine. The oasis became his sanctuary, hence the name. The spring dried up many years ago, but the name stuck. The town consisted of a loose layout of cheap dwellings occupied by retired folks, misfits, and ne'er-do-wells looking to escape the unwelcome changes of an ever changing society. According to the 1910 census, the population of Sanctuary, New Mexico, was 132 souls. Now, in 1966, the population had dwindled to 89. There was a Main Street that ran out of the town to the north toward Albuquerque, and south to the Mexican border. There were few buildings along Main Street; a few houses, mobile homes mostly, a shack or two, and three businesses.

At the south end was "Sandy's," a ramshackle two-story, stucco, adobe brick building with a bar on the main floor and living quarters above. The building sat in the middle of a large, unpaved parking lot. It was painted pink; the front door was painted lime green. There were two windows, one on either side of the green door, both decorated by the requisite neon beer signs. One worked, the other didn't. The sign above the door read "Sandy's Bar and Mexican Cuisine." Sandy's was a busy place Friday and Saturday nights, but not for the food. Sandy's was a rough joint, often visited by the county sheriff, but not for the drink. If the old prospector who named Sanctuary was to come back today, he would certainly have changed the name after an hour or two at Sandy's on a Saturday night.

Halfway up Main Street to the north and on the opposite side of the street was the Sanctuary Hardware. This old building, badly in need of paint; any paint, any color, was an anomaly. It would have fit better in any small Midwestern town. Built of lumber in the mid-nineteenth century style, it was a long, narrow shed-like structure with a false front that made it look grander than it was. It had been a tavern before the turn of the century. It would probably do better as a tavern now, but it served the locals well as the town hardware. Nobody wanted to drive to Albuquerque to get a pound of nails and, as folks know, everybody needs a pound of nails.

The old building was the last of its kind in this slowly dying town, bypassed by the modern world. The Main Street was lined by copies of this building in days gone by. Now, it was the only one left. It still retained its "Old West" charm with wooden floors and a pressed tin ceiling. It still had the fancy old bar from its saloon days, worn, dirty, and damaged. The owner used it as his sales counter.

At the north end of Main Street stood the last of Sanctuary's business district; "Franky's Friendly Fill-up and Fodder." This was Sanctuary's combination gas station and grocery store. Like Sandy's, it was a two-story, adobe brick building with stucco, but painted white. It sat in the middle of a large, paved parking lot with a large awning covering two gas pumps that served both regular and high-test gas. There was an air pump available at the north front corner of the lot. You could check your tires and fill them for a dime. If you needed kerosene, there was a pump in the back. If you needed diesel, there was a pump in the back for that, too. But Frank didn't sell much diesel; not many semis came through Sanctuary. The awning over the gas pumps extended to the front of the building, which also served as the town's only grocery store. Nobody wanted to drive to Albuquerque for a gallon of milk and, as folks know, everybody needs a gallon of milk.

This adobe building was larger than the one that housed Sandy's Bar and Mexican Cuisine. Like Sandy's, there were two windows at the front of the building, in the shadow of the big awning. Both had been enlarged at one time to make the building more open and appealing to customers. Between the windows was the entrance to the store, a set of wooden double doors, one labeled "in," the other "out." The doors were separated by a single vertical frame piece, also made of wood. The door labeled "in" had a little bell hung above it on a spring, so that when the door was opened, it hit the bell, announcing the entrance of a customer.

Franky had intended to replace the doors with modern metal and glass doors, but just had not gotten around to it. The inside of the store was a pretty typical, small grocery store; a large rectangular room with aisles running parallel with the length of the room. In the front, inside the double doors, was a sizable open area that allowed Franky to arrange various display units showcasing weekly specials, candy bars, and magazines. Also at the front of the store was the sales counter.

Franky's sales counter was a wooden bar in a large hollow square design that allowed customers to check-out their purchases on both sides of the bar, while Franky assisted them from inside the square. There was an opening on one side of the counter that allowed entrance into the sales area.

The length of the building was divided into two rooms; the front, public area, with the aisles, and a second room in back for storage. The storage room occupied about a fourth of the total lower floor. The stairway to the second floor, the living area, was also in the storage room.

There was a large, neon sign on a pole at the front of the lot by the road that read, "Franky's Friendly Fill-Up and Fodder."

Every once in a while, Franky had a problem with the name of the place; people would stop in for gas and think they could get a ready-to-go sandwich or something. But Franky didn't sell ready-to-go food. So folks would come in looking for a sandwich and Franky would apologize for the misunderstanding and tell them they were welcome to buy some buns and a half pound of ham and make some sandwiches. He even invited them to a picnic table he kept beside the front of the building next to the front door, for just such situations. Some folks even took him up on the offer.

The thing was, Franky didn't care if the name of the place was a little confusing to some folks; he liked the name and wouldn't change it for anything. You see, Mildred named the place when they first bought it after the war. Mildred was Franky's wife.

• • •

They got married right after he came home from Europe in 1945. He had been gone for three years; several months in England, then a year in North Africa, followed by nearly two years in Sicily and Italy. Franky had seen it all; the fighting, the shelling, the bombing, the killing. He had seen his best friend blown to bits by a German bomb on the Anzio Beachhead. He had seen dead civilians, dead Germans, dead Italians, and too many dead Americans.

He wrote home to Mildred every chance he got, and he told her what he had seen, but not the part about the killing and the dead. He told her about the beautiful water of the Mediterranean and the ancient Italian architecture. He told her about the cold North African desert and the colorful sunsets over the Atlas Mountains, and the sand. He told her about visiting the famous cities of the Renaissance: Milan, Florence, Naples, and Rome. But he never told her about the killing and the dead, not even after he came home.

Mildred hadn't known Franky very long before he was shipped out; it was a kind of whirlwind romance. They had been dating for several weeks when he got word his unit was leaving for England. So, he "popped the question," and Mildred said "Yes." She liked him a lot, but she wasn't sure she loved him, and she really wasn't sure about getting married. Maybe it was because she was young and had stars in her eyes. Maybe it was because everybody was doing it. Maybe it was because she was a little rebellious and her parents didn't want her to get married. Whatever the reason, she said "Yes." And she stuck by her word and she waited for Franky to come home and then she married him.

Of course, he wasn't the same Franky she had met three years earlier. He was quieter and didn't laugh much. He got angry quickly and there were times he would just sit and stare. They lived in an apartment in Albuquerque for a little over a year, but Franky hated the hustle and bustle of the city and the noise really bothered him, so they started to look for a place far away from the city. They found Sanctuary.

Franky stood in front of the old run-down adobe brick building and smiled. He had ambition and he saw promise. It would take work, a lot of work, but he knew he could do it. It was in terrible shape so it was cheap. They bought it and they worked hard together to make it work and to make their marriage work. And, after a while, Mildred realized she really loved Franky. That had been over twenty years ago.

Franky had been working in the store when he heard a loud thump from upstairs. He ran back through the storeroom of the grocery and up the steps to the kitchen. Mildred was lying on the floor in front of the open refrigerator; she had been fixing their lunch. He tried to wake her up, but couldn't. He called the county volunteer fire department, but he already knew she was gone; he had seen death before.

The doctor said it was an aneurysm, whatever that was. The doctor said Mildred didn't suffer and probably died so quickly, she didn't even know it was happening. The doctor said that there wasn't anything Franky could have done to prevent it or to save her. The doctor said that Mildred would have died if she were living in the desert or right next door to the hospital in Albuquerque; it wouldn't have made any difference. Franky wasn't so sure, so he carried that guilt with him. He had made her come to Sanctuary. This place had been his dream, his obsession, not hers. He would never get over it, and he would never stop missing her. That was a little over a year ago.

Mildred named the place, "Franky's Friendly Fill-Up and Fodder." He would never change it, no matter how many folks were confused. It would be "Franky's Friendly Fill-Up and Fodder" as long as he lived.

• • •

Anthony left the trail where it ended at the highway that was Sanctuary's Main Street, just across from Sandy's parking lot. He had stopped several yards before the end of the trail and carefully studied Sandy's place before going out onto the highway. It looked safe; nobody was sitting out on the steps in front of Sandy's or in the several old lawn chairs scattered around the door. That was good, real good. Anthony went out onto the berm of the highway and headed into town.

Franky was stocking canned soup when the little bell above the double doors at the entrance of the store jingled. He stopped stacking cans and walked down the aisle to the checkout counter to see who came in. Just as he got to the counter, Anthony Caputo clomped up the aisle on the other side of the counter. "Anthony! Hello!" called Franky as the massive man passed by the counter.

"Hi, Franky," came the reply.

Anthony went back and forth, up and down the aisles gathering groceries. He didn't use a cart or basket that Franky provided for customers, but gathered armfuls of groceries and delivered them to the checkout counter. Franky watched passively, sitting on a tall stool behind the counter. He had seen this process before and knew not to suggest a cart or basket. Anthony was very particular about each can and each cardboard box he picked up, checking the label, the brand name, and the content of each, almost as though he had a personal relationship with each one. It took some time.

He tended to concentrate on soups, canned fruits and vegetables, spaghetti and pasta, macaroni and cheese; always non-perishables. Then he would get apples and potatoes, and a loaf of bread. He had to be careful not to get too much; everything he bought, he had to carry eight miles home again. Franky could count on the Caputos to stop in at least once a week.

Usually Anthony's father Angelo Caputo was the one to buy the groceries. Occasionally Arlene, Anthony's mother stopped, but she had been pretty sick, or so Franky had heard. When Arlene had stopped, Anthony was always with her, never with Angelo, however. The last several weeks had been different; Anthony came by himself. Franky had not seen Angelo nor Arlene for some time.

Anthony finished stacking his grocery choices on the counter and stood, rocking back and forth from one foot to the other, waiting for Franky to add it all up.

"How ya doin', Anthony?" asked Franky.

"Anthony is good," was the reply.

"So, how's your ma? I heard she was sick," asked Franky.

"Mama's sleeping," said Anthony.

Franky stopped working with the groceries and looked at Anthony for a second. What an odd reply, he thought. Well, it is Anthony, he thought. He shrugged and continued adding up the food.

"And your Pa? I haven't seen him around, he okay? He hasn't been in for a while," said Franky.

"Papa's sleeping," was the answer.

Franky looked up at Anthony again and just shook his head. "Okay, Anthony, your total is thirty-seven dollars and fifty cents."

Anthony looked at Franky with a troubled expression. He was still rocking back and forth from one foot to the next. He looked off into space and began digging into his pockets. Finally he produced a piece of paper from one of the hip pockets of his overalls. He unfolded the paper, a check, smoothed it out on the counter and handed it to Franky.

The check was a County Subsistence payment check made out to Angelo Caputo. It was a monthly welfare check for the amount of one hundred and twenty dollars.

Franky was not surprised; this happened pretty often. There wasn't a bank in Sanctuary. The closest bank was in Albuquerque. Locals would come in at the beginning of the month and buy groceries for a couple weeks, then hand their Social Security check to Franky. Sometimes they would ask for the difference, sometimes they would tell him to keep the whole amount and credit it to the next time they came in. Sometimes, they would be short. They would beg Franky to "spot" them the difference until they could pay him the balance. Sometimes he would make them put groceries back, sometimes he would just say, "Okay."

Franky had seen the killing and the dead, he had seen suffering and hardship; he would not be one to add to it. He knew he would never be rich, at least financially. It was okay, he was getting by.

Anthony was carefully packing his purchases in the old Boy Scout knapsack. Some went into his pockets. All of a sudden, he looked up. "Anthony forgot!" as he went over to the refrigerated dairy case and took out a quart of milk and brought it back to the counter.

Franky added it to the bill, "You want some Paydays?" he asked.

Anthony's eyes lit up, "Oh, Franky! You got Paydays?" His agitation became pronounced, his hopping from foot to foot accelerated and he grinned broadly.

"Of course I do, Anthony! I know you like 'em, I keep a supply on hand just for you!"

"Uh, thank you, Franky!"

Franky reached under the counter and came up with a box of a dozen Paydays. He put them on the counter for Anthony to pack away. He thoughtfully studied Anthony for a moment.

"How ya doin', Anthony? Everything okay at home? I haven't seen your parents for a while, you sure they're okay" He was repeating himself, but he thought he might get a bit more information. Something didn't seem right.

"Okay! Yeah, okay! Mama's sleeping, Papa's sleeping! Yeah, yeah, okay!" Was Anthony's reply, still rocking back and forth.

Franky leaned on the counter, his hands spread apart, looking down at the worn wooden surface.

"Okay, Anthony." He sighed. "Hey, you goin' home on the trail past Sandy's?" he asked, looking up at Anthony.

"Uhh, yeah."

"Now, you know you're taking a chance Sandy or one of his boys'll see ya. Why don't you take the trail around the back of town?"

Anthony looked down at the floor, embarrassed, "Anthony's scared," he said.

"Scared! What on earth could someone your size be scared of?' asked Franky.

"Ghost!"

"Anthony," began Franky, exasperated. "Look, you know there is no such thing as ghosts! That old story of the ghost of the 'Sanctuary prospector' haunting that trail is just BS...you know that!"

Anthony nodded his head up and down, "Anthony knows; no such thing as ghosts. Anthony's scared!"

"Ahh, go on, get outta here!" Franky waved his hands in the air at Anthony, "I'll keep the balance from the check as credit the next time you're in. Anthony, just watch out for Sandy and his boys, will ya?"

"Okay, Franky, okay!" Anthony picked up the stuffed knapsack with one hand and the quart of milk with the other and turned for the door. He made an odd spectacle going out through the double front doors of the store; torn white t-shirt, knee-height cut-off overalls, pockets bulging with canned goods, dirty feet sticking out of the trashed Converse tennis shoes. He carried the knapsack in his left hand and the quart of milk in his right.

It was eight miles back to the ranch in ninety-plus degree heat; a three-hour trek. Anthony knew the milk wouldn't make it so he would drink the whole quart along the way. He walked south along Main Street toward Sandy's to the trail back to the ranch. He kept an eye out for Sandy or any of his boys, but he was in luck, this time; nobody was sitting outside of Sandy's as he passed by. He took the trail across from Sandy's back to the ranch.

There were two trails that led from the town of Sanctuary to the base of the rim of the mesa near the Caputo property. One of the trails came out on the highway across from Sandy's Bar and Grill. The other went behind the hardware several hundred yards, past the rock outcropping that legend said was the place of the spring where the prospector found sanctuary over a hundred years ago. People being people, over time, a legend grew about the rock outcropping being haunted by the ghost of the old prospector.

Anthony never took the trail past the prospector's sanctuary; Anthony was afraid.

Anthony arrived at the Caputo ranch around 3:30 in the afternoon. Despite the heat, despite being tired, and despite having hiked back from Sanctuary for the last three hours, he did not take the groceries into the ranch house, but circled around the house and headed toward the ascending slope several hundred yards behind it. He followed a relatively new trail that led up the increasingly steep escarpment wall on a series of switchbacks. As Anthony trudged up the seven-hundred foot face of the escarpment, the environment began to change from the dry, parched heat of the desert below to a cooler, more temperate atmosphere prevalent at the higher altitude. The fauna changed as well.

Whereas mesquite, creosote bush, and tumbleweed dominated the lowlands around Sanctuary, the low rolling hills above the mesa rim included piñon pine, juniper, and spruce.

Anthony's climb required an extra hour of effort, but he did not seem to mind, and he relished the cooler, fresher air as he approached the top of the cliff-face. Finally reaching the rim, he stopped and turned to face the vast valley below. Breathing deeply, he put down his load of groceries, sat down on a large rock beside the trail and rested. He had sat on this rock many times over the last few years. He had purposely worn this trail to pass this rock so he could use it as a seat to rest on while carrying many heavy loads up the escarpment wall. He sat, resting there for an hour, watching the sun cast different colors across the landscape below and the distant mesas to the west as it journeyed its way through the late afternoon. Then he picked up the Boy

Scout pack of food and continued across the crest of the mesa, heading back into the forest of spruce and Ponderosa Pine.

Finally, arriving at his destination, nearly a mile from the edge of the escarpment, Anthony walked into a large clearing of his own making. On a slight rise near the center of the clearing stood a small, rectangular log cabin. It measured approximately twelve feet wide by sixteen feet long. Its gabled roof was covered with sheets of tin roofing apparently scavenged from another building. There was an opening at the center front of the cabin for a door and a rectangular opening on both long sides of the structure for windows. There were no windows or door in place yet.

Most of the spaces between the logs had been chinked with wood chips, from cutting the logs, and covered with wet clay mixed with dry grass for stability. The chinking was yet to be completed. Surrounding the cabin was an open area of about an acre, spotted with tree trunks, the trees now comprising the walls of the cabin. Smaller limbs and branches had been cleared away with the exception of those that had been cut into firewood. Nearly two cord of firewood was stacked several feet from the door and covered with a tarp. There was a large pile of stone piled near the rear of the cabin and a small ring of stone thirty feet in in front of the door, forming a fire pit.

Anthony went into the cabin. It was lightly furnished with a small table and one kitchen chair at the center of the hard-packed dirt floor. An old bookcase stood against one wall with another small table under the window opening next to it. A long pile of straw covered with blankets lay on the floor against the other wall, opposite the bookcase. At the center of the backside of the cabin was an opening about five feet square. Someday this would become the fireplace, built from the rocks piled by the back of the cabin.

Anthony went to the table beside the bookshelves and carefully removed the food containers from the Boy Scout pack and his pockets. He neatly arranged them on the table, making certain that all matching cans and boxes were stacked together. Then he carefully placed everything on the bookcase shelves, arranging each package so that the label was facing out.

After completing the task of storing his food, he stripped off his clothes and rolled them into a bundle. He had been looking forward to this all afternoon. He picked up the bundle of his dirty, sweaty clothes, left the cabin, and walked fifty yards or so beyond the edge of the clearing into the forest where a small stream flowed across the forest floor. He followed the stream up a low rise as it splashed down over rocks and fallen tree branches obstructing its flow, creating a series of clear waterfalls and small pools over and around its rocky stream bed. At the top of the rise was a low dam, built by Anthony a year before, that added depth to an already existing pool of mountain water six or eight feet in diameter and three feet deep, at most. The water source was a fresh water spring sprouting forth from the rock formation six feet further up the slope.

Anthony waded into the water, taking his time as the cold water overcame the heat in which his body had been immersed throughout the day. The water was cold but as he gradually settled into its depths, his skin adapted to the temperature. He sat shoulder deep in the pool, relaxing his stressed muscles. He sat in the pool for another hour, almost falling asleep. Finally, he stood up and carefully left the pool, retrieved his dirty clothes, knelt down beside the pool and washed them, rubbing and smacking the wet clothing against a rock. He then headed back to the clearing and the cabin. He hung the clothing on a piece of clothesline he had stretched from the corner of the cabin to a small sapling he had purposely not cut down. He went into the cabin and soon returned with a large thick book.

Anthony Caputo knew how to read. His mother had made certain of that, believing that anyone who knew how to read would be able to get on in the world, at least with marginal success, and not easily be taken advantage of. He was not schooled or proficient, his reading ability was rudimentary, but Mother Arlene Caputo worked hard with him. His disadvantages made it harder but she was a woman of strong will. In time, her efforts paid off.

Anthony had brought two books to the cabin from the ranch house below. One was an old "how to book" for outdoorsmen; it explained how log cabins were built. The outcome of Anthony's slow, labored study of this book stood, nearly complete, at the center of the clearing.

The second book in Anthony's library was the old family Bible. He now retrieved the Bible from its spot on the bookshelves, brought it out by the fire ring, as it was too dark to read in the cabin, and sat down on a large piece of log he kept as a chair beside his fire pit. He opened the old, worn, leather-bound book to Luke in the New Testament. He studied the scripture with furrowed brow. He was not a fast reader and had a limited vocabulary.

He spent a great deal of time sounding out words with which he was not familiar and for which he had no idea of meaning. But he never quit; he read passages from the

Bible every evening before making dinner. As he sat studying the words before him, in his mind he could see his mother in the bedroom of the old broken-down ranch house. The blinds in her bedroom were drawn because she couldn't stand the bright sunlight. She was sitting up in her sick bed to add emphasis to what she was going to say. Her pink nightgown with the lace around the collar, no longer fitting her, sagged piteously forward of her emaciated and boney shoulders. Her grey hair was uncared for and disheveled. She pointed her finger at him, saying, "Now Anthony, do not forget to read your Bible! You must read the scriptures every night, no matter what else happens! You hear me, Anthony? Now, promise me!" Her voice, not much more than a harsh whisper, still carried an edge of urgency, as she tried to give her only son at least one more, feeble surge of motherly guidance.

"Anthony promise, Mama."

And so he did; at least he tried, faithfully, to live up to his promise. He read scripture every evening. There was little pattern or purpose to his efforts; one evening reading from Proverbs, the next from Deuteronomy, and this evening from Luke, in the New Testament. He had actually enjoyed Exodus, though the word itself meant nothing to him. He liked the story of Moses leading the Israelites out of Egypt. He had also enjoyed the story of Noah, in Genesis. He spent a lot of time wondering about the Great Flood; where did all the water come from, and then, where did it go? He had begun reading in Genesis, but became very confused very quickly. How could it be that people could live so many years? What did it mean by "begat?"

Anthony studied his scriptures until the Sun's setting made it too dark to read. He took the Bible back into the cabin, placed it on its designated space on the shelves, lit a candle, and studied the food selections on the old bookshelves.

He picked up a can of pork and beans, a can of sliced peaches, his can opener, and a spoon. Returning to the fire pit, he dribbled hot wax onto one of the stones surrounding the pit and stuck the candle into it, so the candle stood on its own. He turned his attention to making a fire. Satisfied the fire would burn, he sat down on his log chair and opened the cans of beans and peaches. As the fire took hold, Anthony added wood. He didn't need a large fire to cook the beans; he didn't need the fire for warmth. Staring into the flames, waiting for the fire to grow to his liking, he absently ate an occasional spoonful of peaches. He put the open can of beans on a flat rock close to the flames, spinning the can a quarter turn every so often to heat it evenly.

With dinner over, the beans and peaches gone, Anthony found he was still hungry. He picked up the candle and went into the cabin and looked over the containers of food on the shelves again. He finally took two pieces of bread from the sliced loaf in the cellophane bread wrapper. He stood looking at his larder as he ate the bread; it just wasn't enough. He had been aware of the problem for some time; he was just too big and he worked too hard. That meant he had to eat a lot to satisfy his hunger and that meant he had to bring more food to the cabin. That required going into town more often than he wanted. He could carry only so much food the eight miles from Sanctuary to the ranch, then up the trail to the top of the mesa and to the cabin in the woods. He would have been very happy if he never had to go to Sanctuary ever again. He groaned in frustration as he realized he would have to back to Franky's in less than a week.

...

Franky was replenishing the refrigerated dairy case. It was Friday morning and he had just received a shipment of whole milk, two-percent milk, skim milk, and cottage cheese. He needed to get it into the refrigerator as soon as possible. This was part of Franky's weekly routine. Dairy products and baked goods were always delivered Friday mornings with the knowledge that the locals would need them for the weekend. The baked goods had not yet arrived, but Franky expected the delivery truck any minute. He wanted to get the dairy finished before it arrived.

The front door bell tinkled. Franky stopped what he was doing, wiped his wet hands on the towel he usually carried around the store with him and headed for the check-out counter toward the front of the store, expecting the delivery driver from the bakery. As he got to the front, he saw that there were four men standing by the counter; actually, two men and two teen-aged boys. "Oh no!" he thought as he went behind the counter. One of the men was Sandy Fisher, Franky's older brother, and owner of "Sandy's Bar and Mexican Cuisine," located at the other end of town.

The other man was "Pedro," (at least that was how Franky knew him). He had never heard a last name for Pedro and really didn't know the man's real name. Pedro was a Mexican national, spoke very little, smiled less, and was Sandy's constant companion. Pedro acted as Sandy's bouncer at the bar and was one rough character.

The other two with Sandy were no older than eighteen or nineteen and were local kids who had dropped out of school and had nowhere to go. They hung out at Sandy's most of the time. Sandy kind of took them under his wing, to their great detriment. Sandy used them for odd jobs and errands. Franky didn't know their names.

Several years after Franky and Mildred bought the store, Sandy came to Franky and asked if he would help him buy the old adobe building at the other end of town. Franky's mother was still alive at the time and asked Franky to help his brother out.

Sandy had just been released from state prison where he had spent the war years doing five to ten for extortion and armed robbery. Franky and Sandy did not get along; they never had. But when their mother begged Franky to help Sandy; to give him a fresh start, Franky really had no choice. Franky and Sandy never talked much. Franky stayed as far away from Sandy's place as the size of Sanctuary would allow. It seemed like whenever Franky saw or heard from his brother, Sandy always needed something. As he grimly went behind the counter, Franky feared that today would be no different.

Sandy was several inches shorter than Franky; stockier and heavily built. He had long, wavy, nearly shoulder-length blond hair that matched his name. He was better looking than Franky and had a naturally friendly air about him that attracted people, hence his followers. He knew people tended to like him and he had learned to use that trait to his advantage; he was an extrovert, outgoing, and always smiling. Franky did not trust his brother in the least.

"Franky! Brother Franky! How the hell are you?" exclaimed Sandy, arms outspread, broad smile on his face.

"I'm getting along." deadpanned Franky.

"I never see you, brother! Why don't you come down to my place sometime? I'll give you beer on the house. We'll talk about the good times back home!"

Franky didn't remember too many "good times" back home. "Maybe, some time," Franky replied.

One of Sandy's "kids" was looking through the candy selection on a metal rack that spun around so you could see all the different sides while this conversation went on. He found several candy bars he liked and took them from the rack, sticking three in his pocket. He then unwrapped a Snickers bar and began to eat it.

Franky watched the whole process out of the corner of his eye while talking with his brother, "That'll be a buck, plus three cents sales tax," he said to the kid.

The kid looked at him, said, "Sure thing, pops!" He looked at the other kid and started to laugh.

"Franky, Franky! Come on, you know how kids are these days! They're bums, ya know! Come on, Franky, Fred here has had a pretty hard time. Cut him a break! Hey, he's a local, ya know. He's from good ole Sanctuary!" Sandy said. He raised his voice and said sarcastically; arms spread wide, "Sanctuary! The great metropolis of Sanctuary! Ha! This dried-up ole desert of desperate deplorables in double-wides! Ha!"

His compatriots laughed at his alliteration. Sandy was totally untrustworthy, a complete con man, a failure at nearly everything he attempted, but he was not dumb. He leaned toward Franky across the counter and said quietly, "I'll pay you for the candy next time I see you." Sandy suddenly straightened up, then looked around the store. "By the way, speaking of candy, where's your buddy, ole totally tarded Tony?" Again, Sandy's sycophants laughed hysterically, this time at both Sandy's alliteration, and at his reference to Anthony Caputo.

Franky immediately came to Anthony's defense, "Why do you pick on Anthony? He never did anything to hurt you. What the hell! Picking on the poor guy makes you all feel big, huh?"

"Hey! We don't mean the guy any harm; we're just having a little fun's al! Franky! Lighten up, man!"

Franky decided he just wanted this over and these guys outta here. He looked his brother straight in the eye and asked, "What do you want, Sandy?"

"Well, Franky, I'm glad you asked me that. And, you're right; I do need something from you." He turned and looked at Pedro, who was sitting on top of some cases of beer that Franky had stacked beside the beer cooler. At Sandy's glance, Pedro got up, turned, picked up the case he had been sitting on and headed for the front door.

"See, here's the thing," Sandy turned back to Franky, put his hands on the counter between them, and leaned toward his brother. "I've had kinda a bad month down at the bar. Well, income has not been too good, and…well…I kinda had some bad luck…and, uh…well, I owe some fellas some money, ya see…

"So, how's that my problem?" Franky shot back, becoming alarmed as he watched Pedro carry the case of beer out the door. And now, the two kids each picked up cases of beer. "Hey! Where you going with that?" Franky yelled at them. They just looked at him, grinning.

"Look, Franky! I need several cases of beer…just to get through the weekend. Just until my next delivery, ya know! Franky, come on, you know I'll pay you back, once things get straightened out! You know I'm good for it!"

As Pedro returned through the front doors and headed for another case, Franky came around the counter, intending to head him off. Pedro stopped and squared off, facing Franky. Sandy stepped between them and stood facing Franky. Taking hold of the front of the apron Franky was wearing, "Franky!" he yelled, bumping up against his brother. "Franky!" He said in a much calmer voice. He smiled, "Now Franky, you don't want to start something that would…well, not end well, ya know?" Pedro turned back to the cases of beer.

They took at least a dozen cases, he would check the inventory after he calmed down. He was as angry at himself for letting Sandy stop him from interfering with Pedro as much as he was angry with Sandy for stealing the beer. But then, he didn't know what kind of weapon Pedro had on him. Pedro was armed, probably a knife, there was no doubt of that. Franky thought about it a bit; he was forty-four years old; not old, but not young, either. Pedro was maybe, what, late twenties? Pedro probably had a knife, he had nothing.

Sandy was a two-bit criminal, no doubt about that, but he may have just saved Franky's life. Still, they just robbed him. They brazenly came into his store and robbed him of a dozen cases of beer; just carried them out the doors in front of him, in broad daylight, and laughing as they did it! And he had done nothing. What's worse; they'll do it again.

• • •

Sandy stood looking out the front window of the bar. It was Friday morning, around eleven, a week since he had "borrowed" the beer from his brother. He was drinking his second beer of the morning, thinking about the coming weekend. He was hoping for a good turnout the next two nights; he needed the money. He still owed on a gambling debt from a card game gone bad up in Albuquerque. Maybe he could get even on it after the weekend. He hoped so; the people he owed money to did not have a lot of patience.

Movement in the brush across the highway caught his attention. He took another gulp from the beer and watched Anthony Caputo shuffle from behind some thick bushes along the trail from the Caputo ranch. Apparently, Anthony wasn't paying attention to where he was; he seemed preoccupied by looking down at his feet where clouds of dust rose into the air. "What the hell…" Sandy said to himself, then a broad grin spread across his face. Anthony was no doubt headed for Franky's to buy groceries; that was the only reason Anthony ever came into Sanctuary. If he was going to buy groceries, he had to pay for them. That meant he probably had money on him. In his devious mind, Sandy saw an opportunity to score an advance on the weekend's take.

He turned toward Pedro and the two boys who were playing penny ante poker at one of the tables.

"Hey, Pedro, come here." Pedro put down his cards and got up from the table. "Look who's here," said Sandy, turning back to the window as Pedro came-up beside him. "Why don't you go invite totally tarded Tony in for a drink, heh?"

Without a word, Pedro went out the front door and walked across the parking lot. Coming to the street, he looked both ways and started to cross. Watching Pedro's progress, Sandy could tell that Pedro called out to Anthony, who looked up, startled. Anthony started to turn away, but it was too late; Pedro grabbed his elbow. Anthony tried to pull his arm away, but Pedro was quite strong and held tight. Sandy could see Pedro was talking to Anthony, as Anthony focused on what Pedro was saying.

Pedro waved toward the bar with his free hand, obviously wanting Anthony to come to the bar. Anthony shook his head but started to stumble in the direction Pedro pulled. Obviously, Anthony gave in to Pedro; he dropped his head and slogged along as Pedro led him by the elbow across the road into the parking lot. The sight of Pedro leading Anthony, who looked three times the size of Pedro, across the lot was pathetic. Sandy just shook his head, then turned to the two teenagers at the table. "You fellas want to have some fun, come-on outside. Fred, bring me a couple more beers."

"Hey! It's my man, Tony! How the hell are ya, Ton?" yelled Sandy as he came out the door, followed by the two Sandy wanna-bes. Sandy plopped down in one of the lawn chairs he kept beside the front door of the bar. His two sycophants took two of the other chairs as Pedro approached the door leading a dejected Anthony.

"Hey! Tony! I said hello! What, are ya deaf as well as dumb?" yelled Sandy again, leaning forward in his chair.

"Hello," replied Anthony, still looking down. Pedro released Anthony's elbow, turned, and sat down next to Sandy.

"That's better! I thought you was ignoring me! Trying to hurt my feelings," Sandy said, grinning. "So Tony, what brings you to Sanctuary this morning, huh?" Anthony still had not looked-up. "Tony! Tony! Are ya hearin' me, Tony? Hey! Look at me when I'm talking to you, damn it!"

"Anthony's sorry." said Anthony, getting nervous, looking up at Sandy and starting to rock back and forth from one foot to the other.

"There now, isn't that better, now? See you're not really a dummy, now are you? See Fred! Totally Tarded Tony isn't really a dummy, like you said," Sandy exclaimed, turning to Fred, who sat there grinning. "Are you, Tony?"

Anthony didn't reply. He just kept rocking from one foot to the other.

"So, Tony, what are doin' in town today?" Sandy asked again.

"Anthony wants groceries," answered Anthony.

"Oh, you going down to my brother's place, huh?" asked Sandy.

Anthony nodded his head.

"You gonna buy lots to eat, are ya?"

Anthony nodded.

"What kinda food do you like, Tony? You like to buy food that'll make ya smarter? You eat good food that makes ya smarter, Tony?"

Anthony nodded.

"What food makes you smarter, Tony?"

Anthony shrugged, still rocking back and forth. He looked down at the ground.

"Tony! Tony! You're not looking at me again! Tony! Look at me when I'm talking to you, dumb ass!"

Sandy's two teen-aged followers tittered in amusement at Sandy's bullying of Anthony.

Anthony looked up again, with a low groan.

Sandy sat looking at him for a moment, "Ya know, Tony, I don't think anything you can eat is ever gonna help you get smarter, cause you're just a dummy, Tony! Totally Tarded Tony, that's you, isn't it?" Sandy drank a slug of beer, his eyes focused on the sad and uncomfortable mountain of a man before him.

Anthony dropped his head again.

Sandy jumped out of his chair and went right up to Anthony and looked up, his face just inches from Anthony's, "God damn it, you stupid, retarded, son-of-a-bitch!" he screamed, "I told you to look at me when I talked to you!" The two teenagers poked each other and laughed hysterically. Pedro sat silent, not reacting at all.

The image of Sandy, at five foot, six inches, and one-hundred and seventy pounds, aggressively screaming up into Anthony's face had the incongruity of a terrier attacking a bull. Gentle giant that he was, Anthony, at six-foot, four inches, two-hundred forty pounds, would not have thought to fight back, nor would he have realized he had the power to break Sandy in half.

Instead, Anthony gasped and stumbled back a step.

"What, did I scare you, Tony? Did I scare you?"

Anthony nodded, embarrassed.

"Well, I'm sorry. I didn't mean to scare you…you retard." Sandy said quietly. "So, Tony, you goin' to buy food, huh?"

Anthony nodded.

"So, you got money to buy food, huh?"

Anthony nodded.

"You think you could loan me some money, Tony?"

"Anthony doesn't have any money," answered Anthony.

"What? Whaddya mean you don't have any money? You just said you had money to buy food!" yelled Sandy, again getting into Anthony's face.

Anthony shook his head, "Franky has Anthony's money!"

Sandy stood looking into Anthony's face for a moment, then turned angrily away from Anthony and went back to his chair and sat down, "Dammit!" He said. "Pedro, check his pockets, and be sure to go through that old Boy Scout pack."

Pedro got-up, went over to Anthony and patted him down. He took Anthony's pack from him and turned it inside out. Finding nothing, he threw it on the ground. He turned back to Sandy and shook his head, then returned to his seat.

"What the hell's wrong with you, coming to my place with no money!" Sandy shouted at Anthony.

"Anthony's sorry," said Anthony. He leaned over and picked up the pack.

Sandy sat staring Anthony up and down. "Look at you! You sad, sorry, stupid, retarded, son-of-a-bitch. Look at your shoes; all tore up! And look how dirty your legs and feet are! God, you're pathetic! You need a bath!" He sat looking at Anthony and an evil idea came to him; he grinned. "You need a bath, Tony! Fred, gimme them beers!" He took the two beers Fred had brought out from the bar and stood-up from his chair. Without an opener, he smacked the top off one of the glass bottles against the edge of the door opening of the building with his right hand, then did the same with the other bottle with his left hand. He stepped over to Anthony and started to pour the beer from both bottles down Anthony's legs and feet. "Let's give Tony a bath!" He yelled, laughing.

Anthony jumped back, but Sandy moved with him and continued to pour the beer. "Let's give the big boy a beer bath!" Sandy's infantile audience screamed with laughter. Pedro sat without reaction. Anthony turned away and began to run. Sandy chased him until the beer was gone then he threw first one bottle as Anthony's form retreated across the parking lot, then he threw the second bottle. Sandy stopped after throwing the second bottle and shouted after Anthony, "And don't you ever come back here without any money, you stupid, dumb son-of-a-bitch!" He turned back to where Pedro and the two youngsters sat laughing and slapping their thighs. He spread his arms with his palms up and yelled, "There ya go!" and bowed dramatically. Pedro sat with his arms crossed in front of him.

Anthony crashed through the "In" door at Franky's, scaring Franky near to death as he stood behind the sales counter going over sales receipts. Anthony was obviously very agitated and upset. He had run all the way to Franky's from Sandy's parking lot. He was sweating and breathing heavily.

"Anthony! What's wrong?" called Franky, as Anthony came to the counter, spread his hands on the counter and leaned there, looking down at the floor.

"Anthony angry!" he said.

"What happened?" asked Franky.

"Ooooh, Sandy yelled at Anthony, called Anthony names!"

Instantly, Franky understood what happened. "You forgot to watch out for Sandy, didn't you?"

Anthony nodded.

Franky shook his head. "Alright, well, there's nothing you can do, now. So, now you gotta calm down, okay?

Anthony nodded, stood and began to pace back and forth in front of the counter. "Anthony needs to calm down… Anthony, calm down," he said to himself.

Franky watched him pace for a bit. "You want a glass of water? You're really sweating, you gotta be hot."

Anthony nodded, continued to pace.

Franky went down the aisle and disappeared through the door to the storage room. After two or three minutes, he came back through the door carrying a glass of water.

After Anthony gulped down the water, Franky asked, "You better, now?"

Anthony nodded, putting the glass on the counter.

Then Franky caught the overpowering stench of stale beer. "Damn, Anthony! You smell like a brewery! What is that about?"

"Sandy said Anthony needs a bath!"

"Okay, then what?" prompted Franky.

"Sandy poured beer on Anthony." Anthony pointed to his legs, which were streaked with dirt and dried beer.

"Jesus Christ! What an asshole!" Franky said under his breath, then to Anthony, "Follow me, Anthony. We'll go out back and hose off your legs." He picked up his ever present towel from the counter and headed back down the aisle, through the door to the store room, Anthony lumbering behind him. Exiting out the back door of the building, Franky led Anthony to an outdoor water spigot with a hose attached. Anthony turned in a circle while Franky played the cold water from the hose over his legs and shoes. Franky handed Anthony the towel while he turned off the hose and wound it around the hose mount. The two of them retraced their steps back to the front of the store.

"Okay, Anthony, you need food, right? Let's think about what groceries you need, okay?" Franky said.

"Okay, Franky." Anthony stood silent for a moment, and then began his well-rehearsed and repeated routine of selecting packages, reading the labels and bringing them to the check-out counter.

It took longer than usual as Anthony had trouble concentrating. Franky had to remind him of many of the items he normally bought. After a while, Franky was able to total the purchases and subtracted the total from Anthony's credit from the week before. Anthony packed them away in his Boy Scout pack and pockets. When he was ready to leave, Franky took him by the arm and said, "Wait here, don't move." Franky then took off his store apron, went around the counter and to the front doors. He locked the doors, then flipped the "Open" sign to "Closed." He motioned Anthony to follow him. They again went down the aisle and through the door into the storage room. Franky told Anthony to wait at the bottom of the steps to his living area. He went up the steps and Anthony heard him banging around in the kitchen for a while and running water.

Franky finally came back down the steps carrying a pack of his own. He then headed back out the back door of the store. When Anthony had exited the door, Franky closed and locked the door. He then turned to Anthony, putting both his hands on Anthony's shoulders, looking him in the eyes, and said, "Anthony, do you trust me?"

Anthony looked at him questioningly.

"Come on, do you trust me?"

Anthony finally nodded.

"Okay, I am going to go with you back toward your ranch, okay?"

"Okay, Franky."

"…but, we are going to go by the other trail, we are not going to go past Sandy's."

Anthony immediately started to rock side to side and shake his head. "Oooh, Franky!"

Franky grabbed the front of his coveralls, "Do you trust me?" he insisted.

"Oh…okay, Anthony trusts Franky…"

"It's going to be fine, Anthony. It's going to be okay. Follow me." Franky turned and headed out into the desert. Anthony followed.

They walked single file several hundred yards away from Franky's building through the creosote bush, Franky leading, Anthony just behind, whimpering quietly. Finally, they struck an old trail, evidently not well-used by the wear evidence. Franky turned right on the trail continuing for several hundred yards more. A rise of rocks, scrub brush, and low trees began to become discernible in the distance. Anthony's whimpering became louder.

"It's going to be fine," insisted Franky, "I'm with you; there's nothing to be afraid of."

The whimpering continued, but Anthony didn't stop following Franky.

Franky considered stopping and talking more to Anthony, but thought if he stopped, he might not get Anthony started again, so he kept walking.

They finally came up to the rock formation. It was quite large, covering over half an acre. The trail led straight through it, winding around several large boulders and piles of rocks. No one ever discovered where the old prospector actually found his spring; his sanctuary, but legend placed it around the largest of the rock outcroppings and for no other reason than it was the biggest.

Franky stopped at a grouping of smaller rocks along the trail, shaded from direct sunlight by a larger set of boulders. He took off his pack and put it on the ground beside a rock and sat down on the rock. He looked at Anthony, who stood watching him, an expression of extreme pain on his face. Franky pointed to another rock and said, "Sit down, Anthony, take a load off." He opened the pack and took out two thermos jugs, holding one out to Anthony. Hesitating for a moment, Anthony sat down on the rock with a groan, and took the proffered thermos. The jugs were filled with ice water. Then Franky dug deeper into his pack and produced four peanut butter and jelly sandwiches and two cans of sliced peaches. He handed two sandwiches to Anthony and put the cans of peaches on the ground for later. He unwrapped a sandwich, took a bite, and smiled at Anthony, "See, no ghost, no problems, no reason to be scared."

"Okay, Franky," replied Anthony, tearing the wax paper off one of the sandwiches.

"So Anthony, this is the way I want you to come and go from my place from now on, okay?"

Anthony finished his first sandwich in three bites, but nodded his head in agreement. He took a drink to wash down the sandwich and said, "Okay, Franky." He finished his second sandwich before Franky had finished his first.

They sat quietly while Franky finished both his sandwiches, Anthony staring at the ground in front of him, taking a swig of water occasionally.

"You like peaches, Anthony?" asked Franky, digging a can opener and two spoons out of his pack.

Anthony looked up from his study of the ground in front of him. "Anthony likes peaches," he said.

Franky applied the can opener to the first can. "I kinda knew you did," he laughed. "You know how?"

Anthony shook his head.

"You buy four cans of them every week!" Franky laughed again, handing the can over.

For the first time since Franky knew him, Anthony laughed.

They ate their peaches. Franky took the spoons, can opener, empty cans, and wax paper the sandwiches had been in, and put them back in his pack. "Come-on Anthony, let's look around a little." He knew the more familiar Anthony was with the surroundings of the prospector's sanctuary rocks, the more likely he would be to actually take the trail through here. Anthony wasn't so sure but, with urging, Franky was able to get Anthony to follow him while he explored through the half acre of outcroppings. They spent the better part of an hour looking through, around and over the rock outcroppings. Other than a few empty beer bottles left by some partying teens, there was no sign of human presence, alive or dead. They ended up back at the rocks where they had eaten lunch, and sat down to rest.

"Well, Anthony, see – no ghosts!"

"No, no ghosts," agreed Anthony.

"So, if you come to my place on this trail, you don't have to worry about Sandy and his boys ever again. They won't know you're in town. They won't bother you, okay?" reasoned Franky.

Anthony sat hunched over on his rock, looking ever so much like Rodin's "The Thinker," only bigger. He didn't say anything for a long time. Franky began to worry all his time and effort was wasted and Anthony was going to reject the whole idea.

Suddenly, Anthony wiped tears from his cheeks, and Franky saw he had been crying. "Anthony! What's wrong?"

Anthony slowly shook his head, still looking at the ground in front of him. "Why, Franky? Why Sandy hurt Anthony?"

Franky sat at a loss of words; what on earth could he say to this poor simple, innocent mind that he would understand? Finally, "I don't know, Anthony, I don't know..."

"Anthony don't hurt Sandy. Why Sandy hurt Anthony?"

"I don't know, Anthony...maybe because you're good. Maybe that's it; cause Anthony is a good man, and Sandy is a bad man."

Anthony now looked up at Franky. Franky felt self-conscious; he thought, "Shit, what can I do or say to make it better? I'm not a psychologist. Man, I'm not qualified!"

"Well, look..." Franky was frantically thinking while he talked, making it up as he went, "that's gotta be it, Anthony. Anthony's always been a good boy and now he's a good man...and, and...well, Sandy doesn't get it. See, uh... see, Sandy doesn't know how to be good, so, uh...so, he's jealous of Anthony being good, cause he doesn't know how and he wants to be like Anthony, but can't…so, he's jealous!"

Anthony just looked at Franky for a while, "Why Sandy jealous? Sandy smart; Anthony dumb, poor. Anthony got nuthin'. Anthony tarded; Sandy said so."

Franky stood up and smacked the back of Anthony's head. "No! No! Don't you ever say that again! Not around me, you don't. No! You are not retarded! You hear me? You are not retarded! Don't ever say that again!"

Anthony was shocked. He put his hand on his head where Franky smacked him. "Okay, Franky, okay!"

Franky sat down on his rock, taking a few seconds to recover, "Jesus, I'm sorry I hit you, I'm sorry! Shit, I'm not the one to tell you this stuff; your mom and dad are supposed to do this…your mom and dad! I'm sorry!"

"It's okay, Franky," said Anthony, looking back down at the ground.

It came back to Franky again; he had not seen Angelo or Arlene Caputo in weeks. Where the hell were they? Why was Anthony coming into Sanctuary by himself all the time? Why the hell was he sitting out here in the middle of the damn desert doing therapy with this guy? His parents should be taking care of him. He looked over at Anthony, who had resumed his impression of "The Thinker."

"Anthony! Where are your mom and dad? Why aren't they coming into town for groceries?"

Anthony jumped at Franky's sudden question and change of subject. He looked over at Franky, then back to the ground in front of him. "Aw, Mama is sleeping, Papa is sleeping."

Franky stared at Anthony for a long time, "Mama sleeping, Papa sleeping…" He looked away from Anthony, exasperated. "Mama is sleeping, Papa is sleeping…" He focused angrily on Anthony again, "You don't really think I believe that, do you? Where the hell are they, Anthony?"

Anthony didn't look up, "Mama is sleeping, Papa is sleeping."

Franky was pissed; something was going on with the Caputos; something just wasn't right. Here he was, trying to help this guy, and he was lying to him! He stood up, picked up his pack and pointed at Anthony. "Okay, damnit, have it your way! You're lying to me! Look, I'm going back to the store. You go home, and you go on this trail; got it?" He pointed from Anthony into the direction of the Caputo property, eight miles down the trail, "When you come back to my place, you come on this trail or in your dad's pickup, got it?" He turned and headed back toward the store.

Franky came in through the back entrance and up the stairs to the living quarters. Setting the pack on the kitchen counter, he took out the contents; put the spoons in the sink to wash later, the can opener in the appropriate drawer, the wax paper and the peach cans in the trash under the sink. He went into the bathroom and took a shower. After putting on clean clothes, he went back down into the store, up to the front doors, flipped the sign back to "Open," went behind the counter, and put on his apron.

This whole time, he constantly thought about what he was going to do about the Caputos. Something was up, and it couldn't be good. So, should he call the sheriff, report them missing? That was the proper thing to do. He looked at his watch. It was after two in the afternoon. Friday afternoon, hmm; he sure couldn't leave the store over the weekend. If he left now, he could get to the ranch, check on Angelo and Arlene, and still get back by three or three-thirty. He took off the apron, went around the counter, locked the doors yet again and flipped the sign, went back to the living quarters and grabbed his keys from the hook at the top of the stairs, and went to his red "59" Ford F-100 pick-up.

It took Anthony three hours to walk the trail from Sanctuary to the ranch; an eight mile hike. It took Franky twenty minutes to drive the ten miles, by the road, to the Caputo property south of Sanctuary. From the turn-off up the dusty, dirt road to the ranch buildings on the rise of ground above the desert floor was nearly another mile. The progress of Franky's truck up the dirt road was easily traced by the dust cloud following the red pickup, if there had been anyone to see it. Walking the trail, Anthony would not arrive home for another hour.

Franky parked the truck at the end of the short sidewalk to the porch of the ranch house and got out. He stood looking around the rundown ranch buildings to see if either of the Caputos was working outside. He saw no one, but he did notice the rear end of Angelo's old Chevy through the open door of the shed across from the house. "They should be here," he thought.

Seeing no activity outdoors, he headed for the porch. Up two steps to the porch, he could not help but notice the unpainted boards of the porch, several broken off at the ends. The porch railing had very few stanchions left and the entire railing was gone from the porch at the far right end. There were broken down lawn chairs and broken down side tables scattered around the porch, and innumerable empty beer cans rolling around. Obviously, the porch hadn't been swept in a very long time.

Franky went up to the front door. He pressed the doorbell; nothing happened. He waited fifteen seconds or so, and pressed it again. Again, nothing. "Well, of course; the doorbell doesn't work." He shook his head and knocked on the edge of the doorframe, afraid to knock on the door itself as one of the glass panes in the door windows was broken out and the other was cracked. He didn't want to break it, too. He waited; nothing; knocked again. Then he called out, "Angelo! Angelo, you home?" Nothing. Again, louder; "Angelo! Angelo!" He tried the door but it was locked.

He considered forcing it open, but thought, "Nope, that's the job of the sheriff." Franky turned and went back down the porch stairs and to the end of the walk. He looked around again and decided to check around the buildings. There were three: the shed in which the old Chevy was parked; the stables; a low, one story building off to the left of the shed. The stables was the largest building on the ranch with a long row of stalls down one side; the other side, a large "lounging area" for cattle to shelter in on very cold winter nights. The third building was a tool shed located beyond the stables. It was about the same size as the shed with the Chevy inside. All the buildings were in need of care, with windows broken, missing doors, and raw, grey wooden side boards, long past needing a coat of paint. The whole affair resembled photos used by travel agents to attract tourists to see the rustic, picturesque ghost towns of the old west. In reality, it was rotten, not rustic; pathetic rather than picturesque.

Franky looked through each building. It was as if there had been no one living there for some time; there was no sign of any recent activity, with the only exception being the tool shed. The door stood open and there were recent footprints outside the door. Oddly, about half of the old, rusty tin sheeting of the roof had been removed. A ladder stood against the building and the ever present weeds around the foundation of the building were trampled down.

As he stood outside the stables looking first one way, then the other, he was struck by the silence of the place; the only sound being the wind rushing down from the rim of the escarpment, behind the ranch, moaning and whistling as it passed around and through the old buildings, occasionally kicking up the dust from the ground between them. The quiet and the sound of the wind made chills go up and down his spine. "Time to go," he thought. "There's nobody here, that's obvious. So, where are the Caputos?" he said to himself, "Well, I tried…time to call the sheriff."

• • •

The search for Angelo and Arlene Caputo occupied the sheriff and his three deputies for several days. They questioned Sandy and his hangers-on; Angelo had been a regular at Sandy's. They questioned Franky, several acquaintances of Arlene's; old card club members from years past, and Gus Wilson, the hardware store owner. They checked for family records to see if there were relatives that the Caputos might be visiting. They searched the ranch several times, the last two times because they had nowhere else to search.

They questioned Anthony, but paid little attention to him; his answer made no sense: "Mama is sleeping, Papa is sleeping." The sheriff glanced sideways at the deputy witnessing Anthony's questioning and said under his breath, "Well, what can you expect?" They finally took an old, yellowed wedding photo of Angelo and Arlene and sent copies to county sheriffs and police departments throughout New Mexico. And that was it.

The next Friday Anthony came through the front door of the store. Franky greeted him, "Anthony…"

Anthony answered, "Hi Franky!"

"Heard anything from the sheriff on your parents?"

"Huh?" Anthony cocked his head to one side with a puzzled look on his face.

"Your parents, Anthony, your parents; they're missing…have you heard anything from the sheriff?" Franky knew Anthony's problems, but he was still getting irritated with him.

"Mama's sleeping, Papa's sleeping," Anthony told Franky. Anthony had his arms spread in front of him with the palms of his hands up. He was trying to explain it to Franky, as if his explanation was as reasonable as anything could be.

"Shit! Fine, Anthony! Have it your way! They're sleeping! Okay, Anthony, fine! Go get your groceries!"

At that moment, an older gold colored Cadillac passed by the front door and stopped by the corner of the building. The car belonged to Sandy. All three of his shadows were with him.

"Aw shit! Damn it!" exclaimed Franky. This could only mean trouble, and worse, Anthony was here. "Sandy and his buddies will have a great time; they can torment Anthony and steal my beer," he thought. "…gotta do something to stop that!"

"Anthony! Come with me!" Franky shouted and headed back the aisle toward the storeroom. Anthony came lumbering behind him. Through the door they went and Franky stopped by the stairs to the living space and turned back to Anthony.

"Anthony, you stay here until they're gone. Don't come out into the store, don't say anything. Just sit on the steps and wait 'til I come get you, understand?"

Anthony nodded his head, "Anthony stay here."

Franky turned back to the store. He just made it through the storeroom door when he met Sandy, Pedro, and the two teens heading down the aisle toward him.

Sandy came walking down the aisle, arms spread across the aisle, big smile on his face, "Little brother! How the hell are you?" Sandy greeted Franky exuberantly. Franky knew it was all fake.

Franky stopped mid-aisle, with his feet apart, hands on his hips, blocking the aisle to the storeroom as much as possible.

"I'm okay," he replied.

The three of Sandy's team jammed-up in back of Sandy, completely filling the aisle side to side. Sandy stood facing Franky, a mere foot and a half away.

"So little brother, you still haven't taken me on my invitation for a free beer at the bar. What's wrong, you don't like free beer? Or you don't like the invitation?" The implied insult to Sandy was obvious. Sandy stood unflinchingly, eye to eye with Franky.

"The free beer wouldn't be free; I paid for it. And I like it fine; it was mine to begin with," Franky replied, not backing down.

Sandy stood staring for a few seconds, taken aback by the reply; then, regaining his wits, he threw his head back and laughed heartily. "You are right, little brother, you are so right! Okay, then…a new invitation! I'm inviting you to my bar to enjoy YOUR beer, on the house! How's that!" Everybody laughed, but Franky.

"Okay Sandy, maybe I will come down for a beer. Especially 'cause it's my beer."

Sandy's eyes grew wide and his mouth dropped open in feigned surprise. "Wow! Did you guys hear that? Franky's coming to my place! First time ever! Wow Franky!"

"Yeah, yeah. Whaddya want, Sandy? I've got work to do."

"Well, I thought I'd stop in and see if you heard anything on the Caputo's. Ya know, Angelo used to be a regular at my place; hate to lose loyal customers."

"Angelo wasn't a loyal customer of yours, Sandy. Angelo was a drunk; an alcoholic. That's the only reason he came to your place."

"Well still…" put in Sandy.

"Yeah, still…still he spent money in your place, right? Still he spent his pay at your place when he was working, right? Instead of buying health insurance and medicine for his wife. Yeah, still…he spent his relief checks in your place after he lost his job, right? Instead of trying to keep his place up and make it a home for his family. Right Sandy? Yeah, still…and you did your best to try to set him right, huh, Sandy? Isn't that right Sandy? So now he's missing and you want to know what happened, like you really care, huh, Sandy? And what about Arlene? What about Arlene, Sandy? She's missing too. You didn't ask about her;

what about Arlene?" Franky was pissed, and he was feeling really self-righteous.

"Franky! Franky! I'm not a saint, you know that. Still…"

Giving in, realizing he was wasting his time trying to lay a guilt trip on Sandy, Franky dropped his head and shrugged his shoulders. "Okay, okay…no, I haven't heard anything from the sheriff or from Anthony, who just says his parents are sleeping. Sooo…who the hell knows. I think the sheriff has run out of ideas, so he's given up. Hey! No relatives, other than a disabled son, so, you know what? Nobody cares. Who knows? Maybe they'll show up someday."

"Humph, may be," added Sandy, then changing the topic, "Franky, I need your help…"

"Ahh, here it comes," thought Franky. "What?"

"I gotta have more beer…just a few more cases." He could see Franky was getting angry and frustrated, "Franky, c'mon brother, I'll pay you back. I gotta have it!"

"No!"

Sandy got quiet, put his hands on his hips and looked down for a few seconds. "Franky…I asked nice," he said ominously.

"No! No, Sandy, you can't steal my stuff, that's it…no!" said Franky with finality.

Sandy slowly turned to Pedro, nodded his head. Pedro and the teens started to turn down the aisle, toward the front of the store, where the beer cooler was.

Franky began to move around Sandy and yelled, "No!"

Without any warning or hesitation, Sandy swung his right fist and hit Franky square on his left cheek, right under his left eye. Franky's head jerked back with the impact and he fell backwards into the shelves of canned fruit. The shelves collapsed under his fall with an immense roar and rumble. Vacuum cans of fruits tumbled and rolled over Franky onto the aisle with a continued rattle. There were cans of pears, sliced apples, grapefruit, and peaches rolling everywhere. Pedro and the two boys instinctively turned back around at the huge commotion.

Franky had no sooner settled into the mass of collapsed shelves and canned fruit than a high-pitched, keening scream issued from the direction of the storeroom… "AAIEEEE…" All eyes turned to the storeroom door which instantly exploded outward and with incredible speed, and the mountain of Anthony burst forth like an avalanche. There was no time for any reaction; within a second, Anthony's momentum brought him to Sandy. Anthony grabbed a large handful of Sandy's hair with his right hand and a large handful of Sandy's crotch with his left, Sandy's eyes rolled-up into his head. With little apparent effort, Anthony picked Sandy up, holding him horizontally in front of him, Sandy's head to the right, his legs to the left, and roared down the aisle, screaming the high-pitched keening shriek… "AAIEEEE…"

Franky, coming to his senses, screamed, "Anthony, No!" but Anthony was completely out of his mind and beyond hearing or obeying any command.

Sandy's head was sticking out to the right of the aisle and as Anthony progressed down the aisle, the back of his head, held tightly by Anthony's right hand, connected with the items stacked along the aisle's shelves. Glass jars of beets crashed to the floor as Sandy's skull wiped them off the shelves, followed by olives, pickles, and tomato sauce. Sandy's arms and legs flailed in all directions.

Sandy's two teenage followers had just enough time to turn and run in front of the advancing mass of Anthony carrying Sandy. Down the aisle they fled, out the front door and away. Pedro, who had been standing closest to Sandy, had no time at all. Caught in Anthony's advancing rush and pushed by Sandy's body as if it was a bulldozer blade, Pedro backpedaled down the aisle, arms waving in an attempt to maintain balance. By the time all had reached the front counter, Pedro stepped on a can of peaches that had rolled to the front of the store after Franky's fall into the canned fruit. The can of peaches was Pedro's undoing; his feet flew out from under him and he fell heavily backwards. On his way down, his head caught the corner of the counter, and then he hit the floor directly in front of the oncoming Anthony-Sandy bulldozer. Anthony stepped directly in the middle of Pedro's gut and nearly four hundred pounds of combined Anthony and Sandy crushed into his midsection.

Anthony, plowing ahead with Sandy's body, hit the double front doors like a charging elephant. Sandy, being held horizontally by his hair and his crotch, could not pass though the single "Out" door. Instead, his head smashed through that door while his lower body crashed through the center wooden frame that separated the doors, and his flailing legs forced the "In" door outwards on its hinges, pulling the hinge screws from the outer doorframe. Both doors fell to the pavement with a loud slap.

Anthony continued on several yards from the front doors, then raising Sandy high above his head, body-slammed him to the pavement. Leaning down over the battered Sandy, he pointed his finger into Sandy's pale white face, "Sandy don't hit Franky!" he screamed. "No! No! No! Sandy no hit Franky!" Anthony turned away from the unconscious Sandy and began to prance around the parking lot, still very angry and out of control. He screamed the shrill, "AAIEEEE…" intermixed with, "Sandy no hit Franky!" As he pranced, his arms and hands flailed the air.

Franky still lay among the shattered shelves and fruit. The entire incident, from Sandy's right hook to the weird quiet that now enveloped the store; sounding very unusual after all the varied sounds of screaming, crashes, bangs, and thumps, lasted less than half a minute. He could still hear Anthony, screaming and occasionally yelling something unintelligible, but his voice seemed far away. Franky carefully disentangled himself from the shattered shelves and stood up. He turned and surveyed the aisle toward the front of the store. "Jesus," he said to himself.

Broken jars lay everywhere. The floor was red with tomato sauce, spaghetti sauce, and salsa. Beet juice, a darker purplish red than the tomato products, swirled into the lake of sauces. Olives and purple whole beets dotted the pond of reds creating a spontaneous abstract painting of food products. Cans of various fruits lie among the broken jars. They were ruined as well, the tomato, beet, and olive juices soaking into their paper labels.

Starting to move to the front of the building, Franky stepped carefully to avoid fruit cans or slipping in slop that covered the floor. Approaching the front counter, he came upon Pedro lying on his back, a puddle of red liquid surrounding his head that was distinctly different from the tomato and beet reds that were smeared around the floor. Franky leaned over and inspected the unconscious Pedro.

He was breathing and had a pulse, but his dark complexion had an unusual pallor to it. He was badly injured.

Franky stood and walked to the front doors, but there were no front doors; they were gone. He found them laying on the pavement in the parking lot with the splintered remains of the center post laying between them. Lying further out on the pavement, by the gas pumps, was Sandy. Franky walked out to him and leaned down. Sandy, like Pedro, was unconscious. And, like Pedro, he was breathing and had a pulse. Franky stood up and looked for Anthony. Obviously still very agitated, Anthony was prancing wildly about over by the air pump, his arms waving around erratically. He was talking loudly, to no one, or to someone only he could see. Every once in a while he would look up to the sky and scream. Franky couldn't understand a word he was saying.

Evidently, the neighbors across the street from Franky's Friendly Fill-Up and Fodder had heard the unusual commotion from the store and had called the sheriff. After a while, a new commotion soon arose as two patrol cars, an ambulance, and a tow truck arrived in Franky's lot. The myriad flashing lights drew a crowd of locals; it was the most exciting thing to happen in Sanctuary in years.

Both Sandy and Pedro were put on gurneys and rolled into the ambulance and hauled to the hospital in Albuquerque, sirens screaming and lights flashing. The tow truck hooked onto Sandy's Cadillac and took it to the county impound lot until Sandy could reclaim it. The sheriff sat at Franky's picnic table taking statements from Franky and from the neighbor who called in the incident. The sheriff's deputy took pictures of the damage. Once the tow truck and ambulance were gone and the excitement died down, the crowd began to disperse back to their residences.

Anthony had gradually calmed down. He was now sitting forlornly, cross-legged out in the middle of the parking lot, his head hanging down as he began to realize what he had done. Everybody knew Anthony, so, everybody ignored him and walked around him. When Franky was finished giving his statement to the sheriff, he walked over to where Anthony was sitting. "You alright?"

Anthony didn't look up, just nodded his head.

"What happened, Anthony? I told you to stay in the storage room. What happened? Why did you do that?"

"Sandy hit Franky! That was bad!"

Franky looked away, around the parking lot, across the desert past the air pump at the north corner of the lot and he sighed. "Yeah, that was bad." Then after a minute, "How'd you know Sandy hit me?"

"Anthony saw through the crack."

"Oh, okay." Franky sat down next to Anthony and studied the sad mountain of a man beside him. He asked, "But why did you attack Sandy, Anthony?"

"Sandy hit Franky. That was bad. Franky is Anthony's friend."

Franky looked out across the desert for a moment, nodding. He put his hand on Anthony's shoulder. "Anthony, you're in a lot of trouble, you know that, right?"

Anthony's head drooped a little lower, he nodded, "Anthony sorry."

"Yeah, you shouldn't have attacked Sandy."

"Anthony sorry."

"Look, you're going to have to go with the sheriff in his car. He's not going to hurt you, okay? He's going to take you to a place where you'll have a clean bed to sleep in, you can go outside and, there'll be trees and green grass. They'll give you plenty of food, good food, all you want, okay?"

Anthony looked over at Franky, "Anthony wants to stay."

"Well, Anthony, I know, but you have to go with the sheriff. Just for a while, okay? After a while, maybe you can come back, but you have to go now," Franky insisted.

"Anthony can come back?"

"Well, I think so. Look, I'll come see you, okay? Maybe...ah, maybe on a weekend, or something."

"Anthony wants to stay." He turned his head away and looked down.

"Anthony, what you did was bad; so now you have to go with the sheriff. He won't hurt you. You can ride in his car."

Anthony didn't say anything or move for a while. "Does Franky want Anthony to go away?"

Franky thought carefully for a minute, "No, Anthony, I don't want you to go; Franky does not want Anthony to go away; but you have to go; at least for a while. Do you understand?"

Anthony nodded.

"Well, c'mon, then; it's going to be okay, Anthony. Trust me, okay." Franky stood-up.

Anthony sat there for a minute more, Franky waited. He put his hand on Anthony's shoulder again. Anthony looked up and Franky nodded to him. Anthony got up and they walked to the patrol car.

• • •

"No, I do not want to press any charges against Mr. Caputo."

It was Monday afternoon, three days after the "incident" involving Anthony and Sandy that had trashed Franky's store. He had to close for the weekend to clean up the mess. Not only did he lose the cost of destroyed merchandise from his fall into the canned fruit and Anthony's use of Sandy's head to clean the tomato sauce, olive, pickle, and beet jars off the shelves, but he also needed to replace the front doors. He had not totaled the damages, but the whole thing was a cost he certainly had not anticipated.

The front entrance was boarded-up with plywood and he had spent most of Saturday and Sunday cleaning the food, broken glass, and fruit cans out of the aisle. He then had to mop the floor several times with hot water, cleaning fluid, and disinfectant. He would be lucky if he didn't need to replace the shelving from both sides of the aisle because the spilled food products had soaked under the edges where it would spoil and create a terrible odor. He probably would not have a choice; the county health inspector might require replacing the shelves.

He had been in the process of mopping the aisle yet one more time when the county prosecutor called. "By the way, did you talk with Sandy Fisher or Pedro…I can't remember his last name? Okay, how are they doing?" Franky asked. He listened while the prosecutor told him of Sandy's and Pedro's conditions. They would live; Pedro had a bad concussion and a ruptured spleen, because Anthony had used his mid-section as a door mat on his way to destroying the front doors with Sandy's body. Sandy also had a concussion; he would be in traction for a while, since he had three broken vertebrae, either from being forced through the doors sideways or being body-slammed on the parking lot pavement.

Franky thought it was odd that neither of them were going to press charges. But then he realized that the last thing either of those characters wanted was any kind of relationship with a prosecuting attorney, judge, or jury; they wanted to keep a low profile. Besides, they had nothing to gain by going after Anthony. The prosecutor went on to discuss Anthony's situation; since he had acted violently and because his parents were listed as missing persons, the prosecutor was going to recommend Anthony for temporary custody in the Territorial Insane Asylum in Las Vegas, New Mexico, until "further developments."

Franky put down the receiver. Well, it looks like things will calm down a bit in Sanctuary he mused as he reached for the handle of his mop; maybe the damages were worth it. He continued to mop the aisle.

The carpenters would be there Wednesday morning to install new front doors. He was excited about that; he was having new metal and glass doors installed. He had been planning to have this done for some time, but the money, and the commitment, just never seemed to be there. Now, it had to be done. "Man, movin' up in the world," he mused, as the mop sloshed back and forth across the aisle. Like the old doors, there would be an "In" and an "Out." He had meant to have new doors installed for some time; maybe Anthony had done him a favor. He stopped mopping and thought about Anthony and what he had said before going away with the sheriff, "Sandy hit Franky! That was bad! Franky is Anthony's friend!"

"Humph. So I'm his friend," Franky thought. "Poor guy, probably don't have many friends; hell, I'm probably his only friend! Poor guy! Maybe I'll go visit him in a couple weeks." He went back to his mopping.

• • •

Las Vegas, New Mexico was a good ways up north; he had to drive to Albuquerque, then to Santa Fe, then an hour east to Las Vegas. The whole trip would take almost six hours, one way; he would need to stay over and come back home Sunday. That would be okay; there was no need to push it. He had figured it would eat up the weekend. He had called ahead to the mental facility to make certain he would be able to see Anthony before he committed to the trip.

The receptionist forwarded his call to the nursing attendant in charge of Anthony's case. Anthony had made quite a hit during the month he had been there; the nurse was very complimentary. Anthony was a wonderful, kind, and completely cooperative patient. The nurse indicated that she was surprised he was there at all. In her assessment, Anthony did not exhibit any tendencies toward violence. He must have been very provoked to have done what he had done to be placed in her care. Franky would be very welcome, Anthony had spoken very highly of Franky. She would be pleased to meet Franky, and Anthony would be ecstatic to see him.

The visit went very well. Franky arrived just after lunch. He met Anthony's attendant, Stephanie Michaels, RN, who talked over Anthony's case and prognosis before Franky could visit with Anthony. She indicated that she felt

Anthony could soon be released as there were no charges against him and she detected no violent tendencies. Anthony would need to have a sponsor in order to leave the facility, and he would need to maintain follow-up appointments for at least a year after release.

Franky explained the problem with Anthony's missing parents, and asked what was needed to be Anthony's sponsor. Finally, feeling a bit cornered, but realizing there was no other way, and that he would not be able to sleep at night if he didn't do this, Franky agreed to serve as Anthony's sponsor, but only until his parents were located. Nurse Michaels indicated that there were legal steps she had to work out and that the necessary papers would need to be arranged. Anthony could be released in two weeks, if that worked for Franky. It did.

Franky walked with Anthony around the well-maintained, park-like grounds of the Territorial Insane Asylum. The deep green grass was uniformly mowed. The brick sidewalks were neatly edged, with benches spaced along them to allow patients and guests to sit and visit. Anthony was very glad to see Franky and wanted to show him everything and tell him about everything that happened to him since his commitment. He was really happy about the food and excited that it was served on real china; he didn't need to cook it or eat it out of a can. He had a room all to himself, with a dresser and a chair, but he didn't like that they locked the door every night when he went to bed.

Anthony told Franky that he could take a hot shower every day. He was ecstatic about the clothes they had given him: clean blue short-sleeved shirts that buttoned down the front, new blue jeans, socks and underwear, pajamas to wear to bed, and a brand new pair of shoes that fit and didn't hurt his feet. They had even given him soap and a toothbrush and toothpaste. And they told him that these things were his now, and that he could keep them! Anthony had never had it so good. Also, he really liked Nurse Michaels and looked forward to his talks with her. They met three times each week and talked for a long time. In all of his twenty-four years of life, no one but his mother had ever sat down and just talked with Anthony.

Franky left before dinner was served, but he told Anthony he would be back for a little while the next morning before he drove home. He also talked to Anthony about being his sponsor so Anthony could go home. Of course Anthony was excited to go home, but was hesitant to leave his talks with Nurse Michaels behind. Franky promised to return in two weeks, and then began his six-hour drive back to Sanctuary.

Two weeks later, Franky drove back to Las Vegas. The drive gave him time to consider the responsibility he was taking on. He wasn't excited about it, but he couldn't just turn his back on Anthony either. Besides, it was only for a year and he had known Anthony since he was a kid. In Franky's memory, Anthony had been a good kid. Other than the incident that had landed him at the Territorial Insane Asylum, he did not know of any other problems Anthony had experienced. Nurse Michaels liked Anthony and did not detect any propensity toward violence. It should be all right.

He would let Anthony live at home, where he was most comfortable. He would insist that Anthony come into Sanctuary at least twice each week; one day would be Anthony's normal grocery day. On the second day, he would drive out to the Caputo ranch early in the morning, pick up Anthony, and bring him to the store to do odd jobs and to earn a little money. That would be a positive thing for Anthony and allow Franky to keep an eye on him.

Arriving at the Asylum, he met with Nurse Michaels and signed the papers making him temporary sponsor for Anthony. He helped Anthony pack his new clothes and accessories into a small bag he had thought to stop and buy on the way. On the way out, they again stopped at Nurse Michael's office so Anthony could say "Good bye." They would be back in two months to meet with her again, but Anthony had taken a real liking to her. At age twenty-four, he could count on less than the fingers of one hand all the people who had been kind to him. Nurse Michaels was one.

On the way back to Sanctuary, Franky explained to Anthony what the arrangements would be. Anthony was pleased that he would see Nurse Michaels again and he was excited about the idea of working at the store one day each week. It was the first real job he had ever had. They stopped at a shopping area outside Albuquerque for a late lunch, and then went to a shoe store.

Anthony would be hiking to and from Sanctuary once each week again. His old Converse had been disposed of, and the shoes the Asylum issued to him were street shoes; wrong for hiking long distances. It wasn't easy finding shoes in Anthony's size, 12C, but they finally found a pair; Converse again, of course. However, these shoes fit. Anthony would not need to cut the toes off to be able to wear them. Franky bought several pair of socks for Anthony as well.

Arriving in Sanctuary, Franky intended to take Anthony directly to the ranch, but Anthony needed groceries.

They stopped at the store and Anthony went through his normal grocery buying ritual. Without his Boy Scout pack, Anthony was confused where to put everything, so Franky put it in grocery bags.

Arriving at the ranch in the late afternoon, Franky got out of the truck to help Anthony carry the groceries into the house. He looked around the old decrepit property and shook his head; how was Anthony ever going to be able to care for this dump? He felt guilty leaving Anthony here by himself. Anthony was in good spirits, though, and seemed happy to be home.

They carried the food to the porch; Anthony put the grocery bags on the porch floor, turned to Franky and said, "Franky wait." He went into the house and came back with the Boy Scout pack. After putting the food into the pack, Anthony said, "Franky come with Anthony!" He then headed around the house and off into the underbrush toward the escarpment. Thinking Anthony wanted to show him something, Franky followed along. But when they had gone some distance and the trail started to climb the escarpment, Franky called to Anthony, "Hey, where we goin', it's getting late!"

"Anthony show Franky! Franky Anthony's friend!" He turned and continued up the trail. All Franky could do was follow.

They reached the top and Anthony stopped at the big rock he always sat on. He turned toward the valley and pointed. Franky looked out over the valley where the sun was creating its daily light and color show across the valley and the mesas beyond. "Damn! That's pretty nice," he commented.

Anthony did not sit, but turned to the trail into the forest.

Again, Franky objected, "How far we goin'?" he called out.

"Franky come with Anthony!" was Anthony's reply.

They stood at the edge of the clearing, looking at the cabin at its center. "Wow Anthony, Who built the cabin?" Franky asked.

"Anthony's cabin."

"Oh, really? Your Papa build this for you?"

"No! Papa not build cabin; Anthony build cabin," Anthony said firmly, shaking his head emphatically.

Franky stood there for a second, not sure he heard Anthony right. "You built this cabin?" he said, turning to stare at Anthony.

"Anthony build cabin."

"You built this all by yourself?" Franky was in disbelief.

Anthony started walking toward the cabin. Franky stood watching him walk away, mouth open in shock. After a few seconds, he followed Anthony toward the cabin.

Anthony went into the cabin, then returned carrying an old, worn, dirty book. He handed it to Franky. It was the "How To Book for Outdoorsmen." Franky opened the book which, because of repeated use, opened right to the chapter on building log cabins. It was a long chapter filled with drawings and diagrams illustrating different processes in the construction of cabins.

Still in a state of disbelief and shock, Franky looked at the open book, then back to Anthony. He slowly closed the book and handed it back to Anthony. Then he stepped back a few paces and, putting his hands on his hips and surveying the cabin, said, "Damn! Anthony! You built this…you actually built this! You cut the logs and trimmed 'em, notched 'em, stacked 'em, chinked the gaps… Wow, Anthony! I don't know what to say…"

Anthony took Franky on a tour of his cabin, showing him where he kept his food, the big hole in the back that would become the fireplace and the pile of rocks that would become the chimney. He showed Franky his family Bible and told him of his mother's instructions about reading scripture daily. He said he hoped she would not be angry for him missing his readings while he was away. Anthony took him back behind the cabin, past the edge of the clearing to the stream and showed him the dam he had built to create his pond.

Franky was amazed; he would never have imagined Anthony was so resourceful. He never thought about Anthony being capable of reading, but he was flabbergasted that Anthony could read instructions from a book and be able to transform those instructions into actions leading to the creation of this cabin! He had completely underestimated Anthony!

As they turned away from the stream and headed back toward the cabin, Franky happened to notice an area of freshly turned earth about six feet square, by a tree in a small clearing ten or fifteen feet from the trail. "What's that?" he asked casually, pointing to the dark loamy patch of earth.

"Mama's sleeping, Papa's sleeping," Anthony said as he continued on toward the cabin.

Franky stopped dead, staring at the patch of dirt. Everything that had happened over the last several months came crashing back into his consciousness in one hard, chilling, frightening mass of comprehension: Anthony coming to the store by himself, the unexplained absence of Angelo and Arlene Caputo, the abbreviated search for them by the county sheriff, his own visit to the ranch to check on them, Angelo's pick-up sitting in the shed, but nobody home, and the repeated, "Mama's sleeping, Papa's sleeping" time after time…it all made sense, now. Angelo and Arlene were "sleeping"…is that how Anthony understood it? Was that his way of compensating for their loss? Is that how he understood death; not being able to comprehend it, did he think of it as sleeping?

Obviously, the Caputos weren't visiting relatives; and they certainly weren't missing any longer…they were sleeping, all right…they were in the Big Sleep, the sleep from which you don't wake up. And, what the hell happened? Why are they dead? Certainly they didn't both die naturally within a few weeks of each other…Why are they buried up here under that tree? Did Anthony do this? "Oh my God! Did Anthony kill his parents? Oh my God! I just took responsibility for this guy! But he has no propensity for violence…really? First the incident at the store, now his dead parents…what else don't I know about Anthony?"

Franky ran to the cabin. Rushing inside, he nearly bumped into Anthony in the small, dark confines of the cabin. Anthony was systematically taking cans of food from the Boy Scout pack and lining them up on the shelves of the old bookcase, each one in its particular spot, each one with the label carefully facing the front. "Hi, Franky," he said.

"Anthony! Anthony! We gotta talk," Franky said urgently. "Uh, it's dark in here; can we go sit by the fire pit?"

Franky was a bit uncomfortable inside the dark cabin with Anthony, who seemed to fill nearly half the space.

They walked out to the fire pit, Anthony sitting on his log seat. Franky picked up another piece of firewood and plopped it down on the opposite side of the fire pit from Anthony. He sat on the piece of firewood and crossed his legs in front of him. Looking intently at Anthony, he carefully asked, "Why are your Mama and Papa sleeping up here instead of in the ranch house?"

"Anthony carried Mama; Anthony carried Papa."

"Okay, why did you carry them here?"

"Anthony wants Mama and Papa close."

Franky thought about that for a moment, "Why are Mama and Papa sleeping?"

Anthony looked down into the cold fire pit and began to rock forward and backward on his log seat and wrapped his arms around his body. He didn't say anything, but Franky could hear a low groan coming from him.

Franky let him alone for a few minutes, realizing that his questions were creating turmoil in Anthony's mind. Finally he repeated, "Anthony, why are Mama and Papa sleeping?"

Anthony's moaning grew louder, he didn't look up, continued to rock.

"Anthony...did Anthony hurt Mama and Papa?"

Anthony jumped up from his seat, looked up toward the sky and screamed, "AAIEEEE!" He began to stomp around the clearing, waving his arms around pointlessly, screaming and yelling unintelligibly.

Franky sat watching Anthony's spectacle. Apparently, his questions were going in the right direction; he had caused Anthony to think of things he had pushed to his subconscious. He was now facing those things that he did not want to face, those events that deeply disturbed him. Franky realized this would take a while. He would be patient, he wouldn't push too hard. He would get the answers he needed, but it would take some time. He now guessed he was not going home tonight; it was getting dark and it would take too long to climb back down to the ranch. It would be too dangerous in the dark.

Anthony's tirade went on for twenty minutes. When he finally wore out, he simply sat down, Indian-style, where he was, head bowed low. Franky did not disturb him; instead he went to the cabin, found matches, the candle, and went back to the fire pit. He picked up kindling from the ground around the cabin and started a fire. When he was sure it wouldn't go out, he went back to the cabin and gathered several cans of food, the can opener, and the fork and spoon Anthony had brought up from the ranch house. He went back and sat on his piece of firewood and fixed dinner. After some time, Anthony stood up and came to the fire and sat on his log. Neither of them said anything; Franky handed Anthony a hot can of ravioli and a spoon.

It was fully dark by the time they were finished eating. Franky put more wood on the fire. They both sat quietly watching the dancing flames for some time. Finally, Anthony said quietly, "Papa hit Mama. Anthony angry at Papa. Anthony hit Papa. Mama sleeping; Papa sleeping." That was all he said. He stood up, went to the cabin and came back with a blanket and gave it to Franky. Then he went back into the cabin and Franky didn't see him again until morning.

Franky spent the night by the fire, adding more wood as it died down. It wasn't cold, but he wrapped the blanket around himself to keep out the night chill. Dozing fitfully, he considered the situation during his waking moments. Obviously, Anthony had murdered his father, probably in a fit of uncontrolled passion, and he had done it because his father apparently had struck his mother. Chances were, Angelo was drop dead drunk. Franky knew there was probably some abuse going on at the Caputo house, but he didn't know for sure. There had been rumors, but it was something people just didn't talk about.

Everybody knew Angelo was a drunk. Not everybody knew what happened when Angelo went home drunk. What did Arlene endure over the years? What did Anthony endure…see…over the years? My God…what was life like for these people? Arlene was sick. How sick, Franky didn't know. So, Angelo hit Arlene, probably when drunk. She was sick, weak, and he hit her hard; maybe he hit her with something…anyway, it killed her. And Anthony saw Angelo hit his mother. Anthony lost control, just like he did when Sandy hit Franky in the store.

So, Anthony hit Angelo, either trying to protect his mother, or in retaliation for Angelo hitting Arlene. Anthony is huge; it pretty easy to imagine the force of Anthony's impact, especially if he has lost all control. Now, Arlene is sleeping, and Angelo is sleeping. Anthony calms down and sees what he has done and is remorseful. They are his parents, his only family. He carefully brings each of them to his cabin, his sanctuary, and buries them here, because he wants them to be close.

"Should I call the sheriff, tell him where the Caputos are, and what happened to them? They'll lock up Anthony again, but this time for good; there won't be any getting back out after a few months and going home. And the place they take him this time won't be nearly as nice as the last place. There will be bars, and locks, and barbed wire…and there won't be a Nurse Michaels. There would be no friends, no forest, or desert, no sitting on a rock watching the sun paint colors across the distant landscape, no cabin, no bathing in a cool mountain stream."

"If I don't turn him in, who will know? The missing Caputos are a closed case as far as the authorities are concerned. Anthony is their only relative, he knows where they are, and nobody else cares. Anthony probably didn't mean to kill his father; it was more of an accident committed in a fit of passion; manslaughter at worst. I can watch out for Anthony, keep him in food and clothes, give him an occupation and purpose. That would certainly be better than what happens to him if I turn him in. Besides, who knows the Caputos are buried here? I know, Anthony knows; that's all, and we're the only ones who ever need to know. The poor, damn, dumb, son-of-a-bitch…his whole life's been nothin' but tragedy! Maybe I can make it a little better."

When morning finally came, Franky was laying on the ground beside the fire pit, rolled up in the blanket. Anthony came out of the cabin and walked over to Franky. He leaned over and shook Franky's shoulder. Franky jumped, then settled back on the ground, "Hi Anthony, how ya doin'?"

"Anthony's good."

"Jeez, I gotta get goin! It's Monday; I gotta get home and get the store open!" Franky rolled over onto his stomach and pushed himself up. He wadded up the blanket and handed it to Anthony. He leaned-over, putting his hands on his knees and thought for a moment. "Okay, it's

Monday; you need to be down at the ranch house around this time on Thursday. Got it? Don't forget! That's the day you start workin' for me, okay?"

Anthony nodded his head enthusiastically, "Anthony not forget!"

"I'll be there to pick you up; you're not walking to the store that day, okay?"

Anthony nodded again.

Franky looked at the cabin, "Anthony, you did an amazing job with this cabin! It's great! Good job! I'm proud of ya!" He slapped Anthony on the shoulder. Looking at the cabin for a minute, he finally said, "Ya know, I'll bet I can get some windows for ya pretty cheap, and I'll bring some forty pound bags of mortar mix with me on Thursday; you can bring them up. You need them and start putting up the chimney, okay?

"Okay, Franky!"

"Okay, Anthony, I'll see you Thursday." And he turned and started toward the trail down to the ranch.

• • •

Sandy disappeared! He had been discharged from the hospital after eight weeks of traction because of his broken vertebrae, followed by three weeks of physical therapy. Franky called to see how his brother was doing and was told that Sandy had been discharged several days prior to Franky's inquiry. Franky called the sheriff and was told that Sandy had claimed his Cadillac. There was no further information; Sandy had left no forwarding address at either location.

Franky was frustrated but not surprised. Apparently, Sandy was finished with Sanctuary and had moved on to more lucrative opportunities. Either that, or Sandy was afraid all the commotion had drawn too much attention to him and he felt uncomfortable and threatened in Sanctuary. Franky was certain that, like a bad penny, Sandy would turn up again in the future, especially if he needed Franky's help.

The whereabouts of Pedro was easier to track. He, too had been discharged from the hospital, but he had not disappeared. It seems Pedro was a wanted man in Juarez, Mexico. There was an outstanding warrant for his arrest on multiple charges: drugs, assault, and illegal weapons headed the rather lengthy list. He had come to Sanctuary to hide out and Sandy had covered for him.

When the county sheriff came to investigate the violent incident at Franky's, during which Anthony used Pedro as a door mat, the fact there seemed to be no real information as to who Pedro really was, alerted the sheriff there might be an issue. He took the initiative to investigate further. Upon Pedro's release from the hospital, U.S. Customs and Border Patrol were there to greet him. He was locked up in El Paso, waiting to see what U.S. and Mexican officials wanted to do with him.

As Franky sat watching Anthony sweep the aisles of the store, he began thinking of the future: his future and Anthony's future. There were opportunities to consider: with Sandy's disappearance, no one was paying the bills at Sandy's Bar and Mexican Cuisine. Eventually, the property would fall into receivership and would come up for sheriff's sale. With a little planning and careful observation, Franky could buy the place and turn it into something of value. It was an opportunity and Franky was a man of forethought and initiative.

Soon, the Caputo ranch would become available. Franky had been thinking of the possibilities of acquiring the place and turning it into a dude ranch. He would completely renovate and expand the house, add air conditioning and surround the structure with covered decks. He would fix up the stables and sheds, install new fencing, and pave the lane. He would need to buy a few horses to start with; then, as the business grew, he could add to the herd. He would plant trees around the house and install a swimming pool. Water might be a problem, but he could either drill a new well or pipe in water from the escarpment above the ranch.

He would need to hire someone to manage the property, and a cook, a very good cook, and a general housekeeper. There would have to be a stable manager and riding instructor; someone who knew horses well. Anthony could find a job and a role there too; he could clean the pool, feed and brush the horses, with oversight. He would probably be very good and gentle with the horses; they would find him to be kind and trustworthy. He could also keep the fences tight and the outbuildings painted, the weeds cut, and the stables clean. He had talent and ability; he had built a log cabin a by himself. Anthony would be at home, where his mother had lived. He could find happiness, contentment, and purpose.

The more Franky thought about it, the more he became committed to it. He would get a loan and buy the ranch. It would be a lot of work, but, in time, well worth it. He would advertise locally, of course. But the real attraction would be with eastern city folks; businessmen, wealthy people who liked the "Old West," who watched John Wayne films and Clint Eastwood movies. Interested people would be those who needed to get away from traffic, honking horns, tall buildings; the chaos of city life, even if for just a week or two.

They would come to learn to ride, or just to be around the horses. They would come to hike in the forest on the escarpment, above the ranch, or just to lay around the pool, enjoying the quiet; and eat really good Mexican food. They would come to sit on the benches he would place at the top of the trail, and they would watch the late afternoon sun play different colors across the valley below and on the mesas far to the west. They would come and they would find…well; they would find Sanctuary.

About the Author

Christopher Craft is a life-long educator; having taught secondary school art and American History for thirty-one years and ceramics for nine years as an adjunct professor at Malone University. He was the co-creator and director of the Artful Living and Learning Program, an early childhood arts immersion program designed to stimulate creativity and improve academic achievement for preschool children. Since 2008, Artful Living and Learning has provided daily lessons in visual art, drama, dance, and music to over eighteen hundred preschool children annually, in public schools throughout Ohio's Stark and Carroll Counties.

Mr. Craft is in his seventeenth year of service with the Massillon Museum. He is a graduate of the College of Wooster with a master's degree from the University of Akron. An active public speaker and amateur historian, he participated in American Civil War Living History for thirty years and was honored to provide historic programming for many local and state historic sites, and the National Park Service. He has enjoyed traveling and backpacking throughout the United States, and internationally. Chris and his wife Marcia live near Massillon, Ohio. They have two successful children and five grandchildren.

Made in the USA
Monee, IL
16 November 2021